THE R FACTOR

**Position Yourself To Succeed
In Any Relationship**
Friends, Intimacy & Family

KINGSLEY MOYO

Copyright © 2019
Kingsley Moyo
The R Factor
Position Yourself To Succeed In Any Relationship
Friends, Intimacy & Family
All rights reserved.

No part of this publication may be reproduced, distributed, or transmitted in any form or by any means, including photocopying, recording, or other electronic or mechanical methods, without the prior written permission of the publisher, except in the case of brief quotations embodied in critical reviews and certain other non-commercial uses permitted by copyright law.

Kingsley Moyo

Printed in the United States of America
First Printing 2019
First Edition 2019
ISBN: 978-1-7770542-0-5
10 9 8 7 6 5 4 3 2 1

This book is for informational purposes only. It is not meant to diagnose and treat. If you need a professional counsellor, find someone who can best discuss your specific issue with you.

Image on Page 87 Copyright :copyright: 2019 retrieved from pngriver.com

All scripture passages use the New American Standard Bible unless otherwise noted. New American Standard Bible, copyright © 1960, 1962, 1963, 1968, 1971, 1972, 1973, 1975, 1977, 1994 by the Lockman Foundation. Used by permission.
Scripture quotations credited to Message are taken from The Message. Copyright © 1993, 1994, 1995, 1996. 2000, 2001, 2002. Used by permission of NavPress Publishing Group.
Texts credited to NKJV are from the New King James Version. Copyright © 1979, 1980, 1982 by Thomas Nelson, Inc. Used by permission. All rights reserved.
Scripture quotations marked NLT are taken from the Holy Bible, New Living Translation, copyright © 1996. Used by permission.
Scripture references marked NEB are from The New English Bible Copyright :copyright: Delegates of the Oxford University Press and The Syndics of the Cambridge University Press, 1961, 1970.

To my wife, Sesu, who is on this journey with me. Together, we are discovering love. To our two daughters Zhane and Zahara who have given us a reason to be better each day.

Table of Contents

Preface i

1 1
   Your Story
      Hello! I Am An Author 1
      It's Not The End 3
      Life Is A Story 5
      Reframe 7
     Grow! 12

2 13
   The Power Of Relationships
      How To Train An Elephant 13
      Disrupted Normal 15
      Invest Wisely 17
      The Power Of Relationships 20
      The Family Of God 23
     Grow! 26

3 27
   Expectations
      Things Fall Apart 27
      Derived Happiness 29
      Minimum Delight 32
      Defined By Expectations 34
      Manage Expectations 37
      Reflect 38
     Grow! 40

4 41
Lost Potential
- What Are You Afraid Of? 41
- Identity Crisis 43
- Lost Potential 46
- The Sins Of Our Fathers 49
- Check-In 53
- *Grow!* 56

5 57
Blurred Boundaries
- God Set It This Way 57
- The Fallacy Of Boundaries 60
- Setting Boundaries 65
- Relationship Markers 67
- How Not To Buy Love 72
- How Not To Buy Love 73
- *Grow!* 75

6 77
Emotional Maturity
- I Am An Emotinal Being 77
- The Heart 78
- I Once Was Young 82
- Emotional Iceberg 85
- Emotinal Maturity And Spirituality 88
- The Mind Of Christ 92
- *Grow!* 95

7 97
  Integrity
    Who Is Going To Be Number 1? 97
    Is Anyone Watching? 99
    Conflict Snowball 104
    Conflict Is Contact, But Not The Way You Think ... 107
    The Way Of The Gospel 111
    Take If From Jesus, Though: 113
    Grow! 114
8 115
  Changing The Odds
    Failure Is Not Final. 115
    Touched By God 121
    Grow! 125
About The Author 126
Acknowledgements 128

Preface

Humans are relational beings. Ingrained in every human is the desire for a relationship. Building healthy relationships doesn't come naturally, it is a learned trait. This can sometimes be a daunting task. The struggle to build healthy relationships doesn't have to be your story.

Perhaps you are asking the question, why is there another book on relationships? In this book, I will share principles that you can use to develop healthy, meaningful relationships with family and friends, including intimate partnerships. These principles can be used in more than one area of your life. This is a one stop relationship enhancement book for all your relationships.

This is a journey of discovery, growth, and renewal. It is an invitation to be real and healthy emotionally. Let's look at how you got here, so that you can find your way to joy and peace. This is an invitation to realize emotional fulfillment.

Your Story

"Only a part of your story is known, the other part is yet to be written."

Hello! I Am An Author

The first thing Jeff noticed were the tattoos that were on her neck. Jeff sees a lot of customers walk into his corner store. Most of them are repeat customers. This Monday evening was no different. Lani walked into his store, just like any customer.

Her accent was unique, and that always got his attention. As they began to converse, Jeff looked at her tattoos and made certain assumptions about Lani. What Jeff missed about each tattoo was the story behind it. A story no one else knew except her. It was a story of pain etched deep in her skin, just as the tattoo had become a part of her life.

Lani grew up in a small town where everyone knew your name. The moment you walked out the door, you greeted people by their first names. Everyone knew everyone. It was a town where stories of joy and pain travelled as fast as the stench of the town's broken sewer system. Her life story was the case.

She still remembers vividly the day she found out she was pregnant. Lani was not only pregnant, but the father of Lani's child was also her own father. She had endured and experienced abuse for as long as she could remember.

Lani's family was revered in the community as the epitome of family unity. That made it hard for her to confide in anyone because she thought no one would believe her story. So she kept quiet. Lani didn't even tell her mother because she thought it would ruin her mothers' reputation.

As the abuse increased at home, she added more tattoos on her body. Neighbours called her names.

Mothers told their daughters not to hang out with her, and all the while, young girls envied her so-called freedom out of jealousy.

Each time people looked at her, they could only see a rebellious teen that had chosen to mark her body.

When Lani finally turned 18, she moved to the big city with her baby. Life in the big city was hard, but better than where she came from.

The tattoos that she had amassed her body with became a reminder of her past that she could not wash away. This is the story of Lani. A young girl who was told "I love you," but never understood that "love is patient, love is kind…it never seeks its own will" (1 Corinthians 13:14).

Jeff, the corner store owner, didn't know the story. He only saw a bitter young lady who was rude to men each time she walked into the store. It was only after he learned of Lani's story that Jeff changed how he related to Lani. And that is how their friendship grew and developed over the years. Jeff had judged Lani by an incomplete story. He only saw a fragment of a picture that was still unfolding.

IT'S NOT THE END

You might have a different story. Maybe not as extreme as Lani's, but still you have a story. The only thing you have left to show for your journey in life are scars and perhaps even wounds that are still open. This doesn't have to be the end of anyone's story. There is a promise, "and I am certain that God, who began the good work within you, will continue his work" (Philippians 1:6, NLT). This does not have to be the end.

Thomas Edison made 1,000 unsuccessful attempts at inventing the light bulb. When a reporter asked, "How did it feel to fail 1,000 times?" Edison replied, "I didn't fail 1,000 times. The light bulb was an invention with 1,000 steps."

The power to overcome lies in knowing that when you fail, you still have another chance to succeed.

Many of our life stories are just the beginning. The ending is yet to be written. God specializes in unfinished stories. The power to overcome lies in knowing that when you fail, you still have another chance to succeed.

You might be still recovering from a rumour that tarnished your image. Your children might have chosen a path that you swore would never happen. And sometimes the ingenious workings of life might have you down after a failed relationship or a lost job. You might be on your third program of study in your short university career. Or maybe you are not even sure what you want to do with your life after being a minimum wage employee for so long. This might be your story, but it doesn't have to be the only story.

> *Hope for a better ending is the most compelling reason to never give up.*

Wolves are one of the most fascinating animals when they hunt. They hunt in packs, just as their grouping suggests, wolf packs. What makes them most successful is that they never accept defeat, even after they have been kicked down on the mouth by a moose. They get up and keep going because they know if they stay down, they might miss the meal that is waiting for them with others at the end of the hunt. They leave their dens with anticipation and hope for a meal. Hope for a better ending is the most compelling reason to never give up.

LIFE IS A STORY

We live in a world that is busy, and it may feel like you are lost in space. Sometimes the room can be full, but you still feel lonely.

And the question may cross your mind, *do I matter? Does anyone care about me?*

As the psalmist once lamented, "I am exhausted from crying for help; my throat is parched. My eyes are swollen with weeping, waiting for my God to help me" (Psalm 69:3, NLT). We are often faced with financial struggles, health concerns, broken families, and the loss of loved ones.

Uncertainty over the future tends to create fear and a sense of despair. Anxiety, depression, and stress become the new normal. Life is full of experiences that collectively form a person's identity, and the journey of becoming is the telling of your story.

> *Life is full of experiences that collectively form a person's identity, and the journey of becoming is the telling of your story.*

Everyone's life is like an unfolding story in time and in space. We are all storytellers, and our lives are the stories we tell. Your experiences of family, marriage, school, friendships, and work make up your story.

At the center of your story are relationships, and these relationships shape your identity.

When God created you and put you on this earth, he didn't leave you alone. He is interested in your story. Life might be a little rough now, and you might not see any light at the end of the tunnel. But rest in hope knowing, the tale of your life begins with God before you are born.

Jeremiah affirms this reality, "[b]efore I shaped you in the womb, I knew all about you. Before you saw the light of day,

I had holy plans for you" (Jeremiah 1:5, MSG). Each of us constructs and lives a narrative; this narrative is you.

> *Your life is not just another story, it's his story. God wants to be the author of your life.*

Our choices can be more powerful than God because God is love and he doesn't force himself on anyone. He respects our decision to write our own narrative. When he created the heavens, he wanted to be a part of that narrative, your life. Your life is not just another story, it's his story. God wants to be the author of your life.

REFRAME

Despite all the chaotic mess that has left us discouraged, and caused ruin and pain, God is still intimately acquainted with our life struggles. The Psalmist says, "you keep track of all my sorrows. You have collected all my tears in your bottle. You have recorded each one in your book" (Psalm 56:8 NLT).

Imagine God journaling about your life.

Nothing about your life escapes his watchful eye.

The words echo through the prophet Jeremiah, "I know the plans I have for you, says the LORD. They are plans for good and not for disaster, to give you a future and a hope" (Jeremiah 29:11 NLT).

God has plans for you and the plans involve hope. Everyone is looking for hope, a way out of that dark corner in life. A step stool to peep outside the window and see the sun rising into that dark place where hope has been lost.

Hope is often thought of as an abstract thing to be acquired or achieved. It is more than that. It is completely reframed in Jesus. It's a story. Hope and your story are two intertwined realities that God has set in motion with a promise attached. It is the story of how God came to build bridges with a world that is in a mess.

The story of how God walked in our shoes, so we can claim his victory as ours.

He is intimately acquainted with your life, in touch with your reality, and meticulous with everything about you. "The very hairs of your head are all numbered" (Matthew 10:30). Can you imagine that? Because of his life, the story of Jesus Christ, we can say I see hope. It's a man called Jesus. Jesus Christ is Hope personified.

If you've tried everything else, try Jesus.

He is the only one who can give you true satisfaction. Anything else will not give you true satisfaction.

> *Hope is rooted in God's promise and faithfulness that he will never let you go. author of your life.*

When people fail you, Jesus won't.

When the relationships around you are not making sense, God will make sense.

You may feel like your situation has been going on for too long. You are tempted to think that God will not come to your aid. Abraham waited 25 years for God to fulfill his promise. "Even when there was no reason for hope, Abraham kept hoping—believing that he would become the father of many nations" (Romans 4:18, NLT). Hope is rooted in God's promise and faithfulness that he will never let you go.

On a hot summer day, a little boy and his mother were inside their lake house. The little boy decided to go for a cool swim in the lake behind his house. He was excited, so he just ran out.

With innocent, tender blissfulness, the boy kept swimming further towards the middle of the lake.

As the boy's mother looked out of the window, she saw an alligator swimming toward her son. Quickly, she dropped everything she was doing and dashed out toward him, calling out to him in a panic.

Hearing the distressed voice of his mother, the boy became alarmed and made a U-turn, swimming back toward his mother.

Just as she reached her little boy and grabbed his arms, the alligator locked in on the boy's leg. A tug of war began. The alligator was strong, but the mother was too passionate to let go of her son.

A farmer passing by heard the screams of the little boy and his mother. The farmer raced toward the lake with his shotgun, took aim at the alligator and shot it. Remarkably, after getting treated for weeks in the hospital, the boy survived.

A newspaper reporter caught wind of the story and came to interview the young boy. He was asked to show his wounds. The boy lifted his pants to show his leg, which was badly scarred. Surprised by the smile on the boy's face, the reporter asked, "Why the happy face?" With pride, he said to the reporter, "These are not the only scars I have from that day. Look at my arms. I have great scars on my arms too." The surprised newspaper reporter asked, "Why are these scars great?" The boy replied, "I have these on my arms because my mom wouldn't let go."

It is also true that God has a grip on you and will not let go of you.

Though life's problems might have a tight grip, God is too passionate to let go of you. He has not given up on you. For all the times you thought you were a lost cause, God was still holding onto you. You may be flawed, but you are loved by God.

Your story is safe in the hands of God.

Just as he spoke the world into existence from nothing, He wants to re-write your story. Your story is safe in the hands of God. He gave his life for you so that you might have an opportunity for a new life. Let him write the ending of your story.

GROW!

1. What is your story?
2. Have you owned your story and embraced it as an opportunity to grow in your journey with God?
3. In your journey with God, what has been the most difficult thing to let go?

2

THE POWER OF RELATIONSHIPS

"Understand the relationships around you, so that you can invest in a healthy and fruitful manner."

HOW TO TRAIN AN ELEPHANT

When you attend any full circus production, you will notice an array of animals that are part of the act. Interestingly, some of the most famous acts involve large and powerful beasts; lions, tigers, bears, and elephants.

The elephant has always caught my attention. On average, a fully-grown elephant in the circus weighs around 10,000 pounds. That's about the size of two Ford trucks.

To keep the elephant subdued after acts, it either goes into a cage or a metal chain. A collar is tied around the elephant's leg and then tied to a small metal stake that's hammered into the ground. This is what keeps it grounded when no one is watching.

Ever wondered why, despite the inhumane experiences the elephants endure, they never try to escape?

This 9-foot-tall, 10,000-pound beast could easily snap the chain, uproot the metal stake and escape to freedom, but it does not. Uprooting a large tree is nothing to an elephant, much more a chain on a metal stake. This is like a toothpick and string to an elephant, and yet it remains tied down by a small stake and flimsy chain. In fact, it does not even try.

How come?

Before the elephant was 10,000 pounds, it was a baby. A chain was tied around its leg, and the other end of the chain was tied to a metal stake on the ground. The chain and stake were strong enough for the baby elephant. When it tried to break away, the metal chain would pull it back.

Sometimes, tempted by the world it could see in the distance, the elephant would pull harder. But the chain would cut into the skin of the elephant's leg, making it bleed, creating a wound that would hurt the baby elephant even more. Soon, the baby elephant realizes it is futile trying to escape. It stops trying and accepts this fate.

Now, when the big circus elephant is tied by a chain around its leg, it remembers the pain it felt as a baby and does not even attempt to break away. Even though the weight of the chain is nothing to the elephant's hulk strength, it does not try to break free.

It remembers its limitations and knows that it can only move as much as the chain will allow. It does not matter whether the metal stake has been replaced by a wooden peg or not. It does not matter that the 1,000-pound baby is now a 10,000-pound powerhouse. The elephant's old belief prevails. When they get old, they don't need a chain. *It accepts this as its new normal, despite the abnormality of the situation.*

DISRUPTED NORMAL

Sometimes the normal we have grown up to accept can deceive us. Is *normal* even a reliable thing anymore?

We live in a postmodern society where truth is a subjective reality.

"You do you, and I do me" is the modus operandi.

This is a society abundant in skeptic minds fuelled by the many choices presented *daily*. The postmodern mind believes that people make up their reality as they journey through life. "I get to choose how I live my life, and no one can tell me otherwise."

In so many ways, our definition of normal is a product of life experiences and the center of life in human relations. It's normal for a child who grew up in a loving home with both parents to see a father as a protector.

> *The way we think, speak, and behave is a social construct found and informed by the many relationships we experience in life.*

The opposite is also true. It's normal for a young boy who grew up being moved from foster home to foster home, to be aggressive and always fight to be heard. It's normal for a young lady who is in an abusive relationship to always be on the defense at work because being blamed is all she knows.

Although we live in an individualistic society, we are still relational beings. Significant to this generation is the impact of relationships to inform our values and identity.

Normal is a product of relationships.

The way we think, speak, and behave is a social construct found and informed by the many relationships we experience in life. Quintessential to understanding an individual is understanding the dynamics of their journey in life and the people who took part in shaping it.

INVEST WISELY

Repetition deepens the impressions, and repeated experiences, right and wrong, become our normal, forming our identity.

No two human beings are the same. Our normal does not always align with everyone because we all come from different walks of life. Sometimes, what we grew up knowing as normal is a dysfunctional kind of normal. Our future relationships are then set up to struggle because we've lived an abnormal life in a normal way. We are caught up in a cycle of broken relationships at work, with family, and intimate partners because we never had the rule book about investing in relationships in a healthy and fruitful manner.

Melissa Gray puts it this way, "People are invited in a crooked room, with crooked pictures, and are asked to stand straight."

A derivative of the saying, "You reap what you sow," is true for relationships. Whatever you invest in a relationship, you get as a return. When you arrive to work late every day, the relationship with your employer will change to reflect your disrespectful behaviour.

> *Many of our relationships have trapped us into an abnormal reality that we need to be freed from.*

Relationships are fragile and need to be handled with care. When handled carelessly, they don't thrive; in fact, they become toxic. It is also true that some relationships, no matter how much you sow into them, you will never get the return on your investment. A wise farmer knows where to plant good seed, the right kind of seed in the right place.

We live in a society that presents itself as normal in some standard other than our own. Many of our relationships have trapped us into an abnormal reality that we need to be freed from.

You are not to "copy the behavior and customs of this world, but let God transform you into a new person by changing the way you think (Romans 12:2, NLT). For Christians, this is a lifelong opportunity to grow. While we live in a society that passes as normal, and yet abnormal, our relationships must not "copy the behaviours and customs of this world." This is the biblical imperative.

Be not "transformed" and not "conformed" to every wind of normalcy that blows around with popular opinions.

As we will discover, the most significant impact and influence in our lives comes from the power of relationships, the "R Factor." Relationships shape our identity.

Relationship—people we are connected with or the state of being connected with someone[1].

Categorically, there are four kinds of relationships that exist in any society. Each of these relationships influences our thought process and reality. To that end, everyone, regardless of age, gender, race, etc., has had an experience with at least one of these relationship types.

Each of these relationship types is like a puzzle piece that helps to synthesize our perception of what goes on around us. They each paint a picture of who God is and colour our relationship with him as we discover him more.

Now let's examine these relationships:

Family of origin relationships—A family of origin is whoever you grew up with at home. It may be parents, grandparents, uncles, aunts, and guardians. For some, it could be foster parents. Whoever was there to care for you when you were growing up is your family of origin.

---

[1] Dorling Kindersley. (2003). Dk illustrated Oxford dictionary. London. (2003)

Friendship relationships—These are the people you tend to call, text, and chat with, occasionally or often, outside of your family. There is an organic connection that is developed over time. Sometimes we end up calling them family.

Intimate relationships — Every human reaches a stage where they begin longing for intimacy in companions. These are partners that come into our lives at different intervals, people whom we date, court, and marry. We open up our personal space to these individuals.

Proximity relationships — bonds that are created by way of being around each other by default; schoolmates, workmates, neighbours, etc. Even if you are not cozy with these individuals, there still exists a connection, and that connection is called a relationship.

THE POWER OF RELATIONSHIPS

The family of origin influences whom we attract and are attracted to. This is the core relationship where we learn all the attachments we've come to invest in during our lives. Only by understanding who you are, can you invest in your current relationships in a healthy and fruitful manner.

Satan's greatest assault has been on the family of origin. The primary reason God created the first family of origin, Adam and Eve, was to give a revelation of the Love of God, "God is love" (1 John 4:8).

The very foundation of God's identity is love. So, when "God said, let us make man in our image...", he wanted to have a continuation of the principles espoused by his identity, which is love (Genesis 1:26). God made Adam and Eve in his image to "rule and have dominion" over the earth with love. To be loving with emphasis on continued growth is God's ideal of our human pursuit of perfection. "You, therefore, must be perfect, as your heavenly Father is perfect" (Matthew 5:48). The relationships found in the family of origin were to be the basis of how you are supposed to pursue other relationships.

Only by understanding who you are, can you invest in your current relationships in a healthy and fruitful manner.

From Adam and Eve, all of humanity would know their "likeness."

The "image" of God was to be handed down from generation to generation.

In the family of origin, there was to be an ever-widening circle of human beings with the capacity to receive and to give love like God does, living in God's "image"[2]. That was the blueprint of God's progressive revelation of love set out for the family at creation. When Adam and Eve sinned, they turned their backs on God, and since then, things began and continue to fall apart.

The family of origin is by far where people receive the greatest influence in their lives, both positive and negative. Most of the things we learn about being normal comes from these relationships.

Neuroscience research over the years has revealed that the brain grows significantly between the ages of 0-5 years[3]. It is also true that the most adaptive years of most children is 3-12 years[4]. From adolescent to adulthood, you continue to reinforce and build on that foundation.

Your perception of the love of God can be influenced significantly by the love you received or didn't receive as a child. Discipline habits and life principles are ingrained at home. The groundwork for the way you will deal with

---

[2] Gibson, Ty. The Sonship of Christ: Exploring the Covenant Identity of God and Man.

[3] AAP Council on communication and media. Media and Young Minds. *Pediatrics.* (2016)

[4] *Ibid*

conflict, financial management, and future relational attachments is laid in this relationship type. If you come from a broken family, all that brokenness can be translated into shaping normalcy for years to come, unless the cycle is broken.

The wise man understood something when he penned the words, "Train up a child in the way he should go; even when he is old, he will not depart from it" (Proverbs 22:6). The home was designed to be a place to learn how to thrive, but that has not always been the case for many people.

All other relationships are a continuation of what we learn at home. We gravitate to friends that are as close as possible to what we are exposed to at home. Fulfillment in an intimate relationship is realized when we see some resemblance of what we grew up with, dysfunctional and otherwise. Subconsciously, we try so much not to relive the experiences we had from our family of origin that we end up reliving them again. It's all a chain with links that connect throughout. It's your story.

THE FAMILY OF GOD

An epidemic that has plagued many people is the thought of never feeling adequate in the relationships they belong. Fear thrives in an atmosphere of felling inadequate. One of the greatest lies Satan has ever told anyone is that you are not needed.

The moment you accept that as true, you have boxed yourself to accept your so-called "limitations" in life.

Nobody should ever feel like they can never be loved.

Fear thrives in an atmosphere of felling inadequate.

Nobody should ever feel like they can never be enough.

Feelings of guilt, shame, and loneliness should not be a constant experience in your life. The relationships in your life were never meant to be a stressor, but to be enjoyed. It's not normal to be moving from relationship to relationship, leaving a trail of heartache and pain.

When you are in a dark place, you sometimes tend to think you are buried. Perhaps you have been planted to bloom[5]. You are not a pin cushion to absorb life's painful mishaps. This does not have to be the end of your story.

---

[5] Caine, C. (2016). Undaunted: daring to do what God calls you to do. Grand Rapids, MI: Zondervan

Jesus' primary purpose in coming to earth was to reveal God's character. To restore the hearts of men to God the Father. To set free all those who have been held captive.

Satan was victorious with our first parents, Adam and Eve. The first man, Adam, became a living person." But the last Adam—that is, Christ—is a life-giving Spirit (1 Corinthians 15:22). In Christ, there is a new life for all the relationships that have been suffocating. As He was nailed to the cross with his arms extended wide open, he gave an invitation to everyone to be a part of the family of God. God has a handwritten invitation to everyone who has journeyed.

> ***God has a handwritten invitation to everyone who has journeyed through life with brokenness.***

God is love. He is loving and desiring to show you something better; that is, a family with no brokenness, a family with authentic relationships, and God himself as the Father.

GROW!

1. Which relationships have had the most impact on your life from childhood to now, good or bad?
2. Which trend of behaviours emerge as healthy and unhealthy in those relationships?
3. Which of those trends have been transferred to your current relationships? How have they been affected?

3

EXPECTATIONS

"The number one cause of relationship breakdown is unmet expectations."

THINGS FALL APART

In many studies, the cause of divorce is money. And depending on which article you read, it can be infidelity. Meanwhile, loyalty among friends is counted as perhaps the number one cause of relational breakdowns. Good friends are expected to show up when you need them the most.

While there are many other factors that can cause relationship stress, the root of all relationship fallouts is *unmet expectations*.

It is true that communication causes misunderstandings, poor financial management paves the way for anxiety, and lack of intimacy can cause relationship strain; these are just symptoms.

At the core of all these disappointments, and many others, are unmet expectations. Each person determines in their mind what they deserve in any relationship. We all have an ideal relationship, and we make up checklists of all the things we desire to see and experience. Sometimes we might shortchange ourselves into thinking we deserve less than we should. This applies to proximity relationships and friendships, and much more so in intimate relationships.

We often feel that people must fulfill the ideal role that we have subconsciously created. No one really settles for anything; we all have this checklist of qualities and capabilities. And we consult this checklist often. Business partners look forward to specific outcomes based on what they deem their partner should do. Friends and family have an unwritten code of conduct that governs one's behaviour in the relationship. Intimate partners expect their partners to deliver in several areas of their lives in order for satisfaction to be realized.

When you don't manage your expectations, life will be a chaotic sequence of disappointments leading to anxiety and despair.

These expectations become the measure of success, and if they under-deliver, the relationship begins to fall apart. When you don't manage your expectations, life will be a chaotic sequence of disappointments leading to anxiety and despair. Things will fall apart.

DERIVED HAPPINESS

The woman from Samaria met Jesus at the well at midday (John 4:6). This was an abnormal time to be fetching water. All women went to the well in the morning and evening when the sun was cool. Something was off with this lady. Jesus initiated the conversation, "Give Me a drink." (John 4:7). The conversation ensued between her and Jesus.

Jews and Samaritans had no dealings with each other, not to imagine a woman speaking to a man.

Jesus ingeniously switched the conversation from water from the well that quenches thirst, "Whoever drinks the water I give them will never thirst. Indeed, the water I give them will become in them a spring of water welling up to eternal life."

This water was not something you travelled somewhere to get. It was something within. The woman says, "give me this water so that I won't get thirsty and ...keep coming here to draw water" (John 4:14-17). Much to her own discovery, she had longed for something better. She had tried men to provide happiness. One wasn't enough, so she tried two, three, four, and now she was on the fifth one.

She wanted internal happiness, which only God could give. She seemed to derive some form of satisfaction by being attached to men. She had a derived happiness.

> *Having expectations that are centred on others fulfilling your happiness is like pouring water into a bucket with holes.*

Having expectations that are centred on others fulfilling your happiness is like pouring water into a bucket with holes. People shift positions a lot, even those that you've grown to trust, whom you think won't disappoint you.

No one was put on earth to make another person happy. It is not anyone's responsibility to make you happy. When you learn your position in people's lives, your feelings won't be hurt when they shift.

Couples soon come to realize that desiring their partner to always make them happy is folly.

Friends soon learn that friends disappoint ever so often.

Even family can fail to come around when you need them the most.

And all this does not always mean that they don't love you; it merely indicates that they are human. Many people thrive on derived happiness, and they are managed by expectations. *Managing your expectations is the key to relationship success.*

Take an inventory of the expectations you have on other people. Be aware of the things that affect your emotional health.

Self-awareness is a relational success key, a trait that is learned and not taught. Having a clear sense of self-awareness allows you to overcome the dependency on others to make you happy. The battle towards your happiness is half won when you begin to know yourself.

The woman at the well had lost sight of her identity and sense of self-worth. Being with these men gave her meaning and identity. Before she met Jesus at the well, she was navigating Samaria in the shadows. After the encounter with Jesus, she dropped her water pot and ran to the very people she wanted to avoid saying, "come and see a man who told me everything I ever did!" (John 4:29). And because now she had a sense of identity, the people listened and "came streaming from the village to see Jesus" (John 4:30).

Jesus left her with a clear sense of identity. She was no longer managed by the expectations of the people.

Minimum Delight

People are shaped by the many experiences throughout their lifetime. With each experience, certain expectations are ingrained in our minds. Combined, all these experiences form the nucleus of what to expect in life. Eventually, happiness is equated with being in receipt of all these things.

As we move on from relationship to relationship, we enter each of them with what I would call a *minimum delight*. Minimum delights are the things that we expect all parties in the relationship to know and do for us. When these things are done, we have a delightful relationship. It is this *minimum delight* that keeps the relationship satisfactory. We respond and react based on this minimum delight.

Some people seek their minimum delight based on a past that is full of scars. These scars define what is expected from them and from those who are in a relationship with them. A young man who grows up being told money is the epitome of success, will believe that the lack of money in a relationship can leave him unsatisfied. Money is his minimum delight. We get into relationships seeking to change, recreate, and discover our past.

We get into relationships seeking to change, recreate, and discover our past.

If you had loving parents who took you on vacations as a child, your desire would be either to experience that again, or you would look for opportunities that will take you away from those similar experiences.

Your professional aspirations are often recommended by family and friends. We pursue certain academic credentials because of family influences. We make decisions to change our past fortune or to recreate the fortune we had when we were growing up as children. Your minimum delight is informed by your past experiences in relationships.

Congruent with this is the notion that our actions in any given situation are influenced by memories of how people have responded to us in past similar situations. We find these memories distributed in stories that shape our day-to-day sense of "self." They are in stories people tell about us, in pain and grief encounters.

We see them as we participate in cultural practices and family traditions, and in many other places. All these memories take shape into who we are and what we expect in life. They inform our minimum delight. Our minimum delight is not an abstract creation. It is informed by the many experiences in the past and around us that we have enjoyed.

When we get into a relationship and find these experiences absent, we conclude that we are not happy because the minimum delight is missing. We then proceed to lay blame, argue, and guilt trip with the intention of evoking change, demanding to receive our minimum delight. If all this does not work, the relationship begins to suffer.

DEFINED BY EXPECTATIONS

Every parent wants the best for their children. But as well-meaning as parents may be, a child's behaviour and performance in life may become a parent's report card

It comes disguised with the words, "I want better for you." Before you realize it, children begin to live a life that is not theirs because of expectations.

The child may even embrace that as their measure of success in life. But in reality, they have become a scorecard that parents use to measure their success.

> *Well-meaning as parents may be, a child's behaviour and performance in life may become a parent's report card.*

A representation of a parent's failure and success, that's a dark shadow of expectations that a child grows under. Living a life with what's familiar and embracing it even when it hurts. The groundwork of what we embrace as children keeps steering us even when we become adults.

As you grow up, you spend your life trying to recreate or erase childhood expectations[6]. Unbeknownst, we become our parents, and the cycle keeps going.

> *Failure is inevitable when we assume what others are doing carries the same meaning as we suppose it does.*

Your identity is significantly shaped and molded by a caregiver's expectations.

From childhood through adulthood, there are many life experiences that have the power to mold us.

They form a cohesive language spoken and understood by only those who have been through similar experiences. People understand behaviour just like they do language. It is a learned trait. For some, a raised palm could mean "hello", and to someone, it might mean "I don't want to talk to you".

When you don't understand and relate to someone's life experiences, there will be a failure to understand each other relationally. People are in relationships where both sides don't understand each other; however, there is an expectation by

---

[6] Brown, Laura S. Not the price of admission: Healthy relationships after childhood trauma (p. 123).

every participant to be understood and to be understood well for that matter. Failure is inevitable when we assume what others are doing carries the same meaning as we suppose it does.

Jesus was crucified because of an unmet expectation. He declared, "My Father is always working, and so am I.... So, the Jewish leaders tried all the harder to find a way to kill him" (John 5:17-18,

NLT). The Pharisees thought he was a God-wanna-be man and accused him of trying to make himself equal with God. The relationship they anticipated to have with Jesus was born from prior expectations, which set the relationship to fail.

When we move at the pace of other people, we lose sight of what God has called us to be. Inevitably, we allow them to dictate our choices and reject the blessing to live differently as God has called us to do. Baggage is laid on us, and this is a sad unfolding of the reality we live in.

We come to believe what others believe about us, and we have not experienced what God has called us to be.

We are defined by other people's expectations.

MANAGE EXPECTATIONS

Jesus taught this principle of managing expectations when he gave the Lord's Prayer to the disciples. After spending some time in prayer, one of his disciples came to him and asked: "Lord, teach us to pray just as John taught his disciples" (Luke 11:1). The Lord's prayer was like a mission statement that each Rabbi or Leader would teach his disciples. With anticipation, the disciples wanted to know what their mission would be.

This was how this new community of disciples would govern itself. Inserted as the second phrase of the prayer according to Matthew,

"Your kingdom come, your will be done on earth as it is in heaven (Matthew 6:10). Expect the atmosphere that pervades the heavenly space where there is no strife, pain, and suffering to come down. But before all this happens, we are still living in a sinful world. Pray that the atmosphere of heaven might come down in its fullness.

Jesus taught his disciples to expect the best but be able to live in the worst. When you expect the best, you give everyone a chance to be who God wants them to be. But when they give you their worst, you already knew his "will" may not be done on earth as it is in heaven.

REFLECT

The mirror is a fascinating invention. It has long been an interest of men to look at themselves in the mirror. Every morning, the mirror can be a reminder of your hopes, dreams, and aspirations. It can also be a reminder of the past you never want to revisit, the person whom you decided to become. The word mirror comes from an old Latin word *miarre,* which means to "look at." Mirror is also figuratively used as a statement of examining yourself. The mirror reflects your image.

You are made in the image of God. God made you to mirror him as his creation. God's expectations are less than men, but their impact is greater than men. Through Christ we reflect God. Even before he made the world, God loved us and chose us in Christ to be holy and without fault in his eyes (Ephesians 1:4). Bad expectations present an alternative and distorted picture of God. Pay attention to the mirror; pay attention to God. Discover the erroneous ways that you have used to see yourself as a fulfillment of people's needs.

In Christ, you are presented "blameless as you stand before him without a single fault" (Colossians 1:22). The Christian does not think God will love us because we are good, but that God will make us good because he loves us[7]

You are only confined by the walls that you build yourself. Reflecting on what God has done for you reminds you that you are loved and valuable in his eyes. No expectation is greater than knowing even after you fail, you are worth something. People's dysfunctional habits are not a reflection of your personality.

> *People's dysfunctional habits are not a reflection of your personality.*

Don't lose yourself at the hands of people's expectations.

---

[7] C. S. Lewis

GROW!

1. What is your minimum delight? Is it realistic to expect that of others?
2. Whose affirmation matters the most to you?
3. Do you feel you reflect God's love through your connections and engagements with other people?

4

Lost Potential

"You will not realize your potential until the damaged areas in your life have been healed."

What Are You Afraid Of?

I sat around a group of young people having some casual conversations about life. There was a question that kept lingering in my mind. I figured that, while I have an audience, I might as well see what answers I would get.

So, I asked, "What do you fear the most? What are you afraid of?"

There was a certain pause and silence that followed. Eventually, one brave person responded, "Snakes!" One after the other, they began to share. As the circle went around, it was evident that every one of them was afraid of dying by so many ways. Fear of death was a common theme.

When the circle had gone around the first time, it came to my turn. I had some sense that superficial answers were being shared. No one wanted to be vulnerable.

So, I decided to be vulnerable, and I shared my fear of inadequacy.

How it followed me for the better part of my life until my early young adult years. I shared the significance and impact it had on my life experiences and choices. Most of my decisions seemed to revolve around being acknowledged by someone. When I discovered this, and changed it, a certain weight was lifted off my shoulders. I was set free!

I then asked the same question one more time,

"What do you fear the most?"

This time with an emotional appeal for candid responses. The silence that followed was different. It was a bit more tense. One brave person followed and shared, "I am afraid of loneliness."

One after the other, they began to share some heartfelt personal struggles of loneliness, body issues, fear of never being loved, and not being able to make their parents proud.

It was at this moment that I discovered that these experiences of fear among these young people reflect some damaged areas in their lives. They were carrying baggage, and some of it did not belong to these young people. They spoke sweet things in the presence of others, even when their mouths were sour.

There are many life opportunities that people have missed because they have felt inadequate. Our reality is coloured by the many positive and negative experiences which present a distorted view of our potential.

> *There are many life opportunities that people have missed because they have felt inadequate.*

IDENTITY CRISIS

Our identities are relational in nature.

God set it to be so from the beginning when he said, "let us make men in our image, according to Our likeness" (Genesis 1:26).

What is his image? What is God's likeness?

Another way to ask the question is, who is God?

The most concise answer to that question is "God is love" (1 John 4:8). There can only be love if there is more than one person to share that love with. The Godhead (Father, Son &

Holy Spirit) is the perfect number for mutual love to be experienced.

One constitutes a complete absence of otherness. Two constitutes a state in which each is the exclusive center of the other. Three constitutes a state in which each one enjoys both being the center of attention and deferring the center of attention[8] God enjoyed an eternal relational existence of mutual love. We were created as relational beings, just as God is relational in nature.

Our private lives are linked to our public issues.

We are not as compartmentalized as we think. Our private lives are linked to our public issues. The relationship we have with God informs our identity, and our identity informs and accentuates the relationships we have with people.

Outside of God, outside of relationships, our identity is incomplete.

---

[8] Gibson, Ty. The Sonship of Christ: Exploring the Covenant Identity of God and Man

> *what really sets the distinction between mankind and animals, ...is mankind's ability to love, be loved, and be loving.*

Adam represented all of humanity. From the Hebrew tongue, his name, *Adamah* is directly translated as "mankind." "God formed the man from the dust of the ground. He breathed the breath of *life* into man's nostrils, and the man became a living person" (Genesis 2:7, NLT). The word *life* is plural in Hebrew. Literally, God breathed the breath of *lives in* Adam, and so all of humanity shared in and received their identity from God.

For the longest while, it has been postulated that what sets human beings apart from other animals is the ability to think rationally. But what really sets the distinction between mankind and animals, according to the biblical identity of a human given by God, is mankind's ability to love, be loved, and be loving.

Humanity reaches his perfection when he has become "perfect just like our heavenly father" (Matthew 5:48). The continuous pursuit of growing to love is our godly identity. Adam and Eve were to have dominion in heaven and earth over the birds of the air, species in the sea, and the animals on the land with love. They were to tend to the Garden of Eden with love. Their purpose was to give a revelation of the character of God, which is love.

Contrary to what we have seen in our society, God never created men to rule over any other men.

Men's relationship and way of relating to God's creation is supposed to be filled with love. The first family relationship was supposed to give a revelation of God, from where their identity was received. God's character of love would be passed on by Adam and Eve to the following generations.

Satan saw an opportunity and understood God's purpose. And he set his evil plans in motion to distort God's character.

Satan called God a liar when he told Eve, "You won't die! God knows that your eyes will be opened as soon as you eat the fruit in the middle of the garden" (Genesis 3:4-5, NLT). On that day, humanity turned their backs on God and sin caused all of us to begin to lose sight of God's love and our identity.

After Adam and Eve from generation to generation, the family unit has been the focus of Satan's attacks. It was an attack on the very institution set to give us an understanding of our identity.

LOST POTENTIAL

Lost potential comes from a distorted view of your identity. If the purpose of a thing is not understood, abuse is inevitable[9] Take, for example, a shoe.

Shoes were designed to be worn on a foot. The left foot to the left shoe and the right foot to the right shoe. It only fits that way, and any other way, it won't work. You lose balance, and quite frankly, it would look funny.

The shoe was made in the image of the foot. Without the foot, the shoe has no purpose. It was never meant to be used as a weapon, a door stopper, and certainly not a toy for a dog.

We carry a lot of baggage in our lives, and some of which we don't even realize is on us. The weight we've been carrying around limits our potential to navigate life with full strength.

We've lost our potential to be the better version of ourselves. Some people grew up in a family that never discussed finances or had a warped mentality of dealing with finances. Now they make good money, but they are living from paycheck to paycheck.

---

[9] Munroe, M. (2008). The fatherhood principle: priority, position, and the role of the male. New Kensington, PA: Whitaker House.

Many people are broken in the way they view other people. They don't celebrate other people's success, and they miss the opportunity to see where God is working in their lives.

We are damaged in the way we view ourselves. Our sense of self-worth is defined by others who can build us up and break us down.

The weight we've been carrying around limits our potential to navigate life with full strength.

Our negative experiences have damaged the way we view God. God's love as Father has been warped by the father who abused you. The enemy has you convinced that nobody will ever want you.

It can be a difficult thing for a person to succeed in any relationship if they have relationally damaged areas in their life.

The upside-down paradigm of love teaches that meeting the needs of others is the price of admission to belong in a relationship[10]. Fear becomes the number one compelling

---

[10] Brown, Laura S. Not the price of admission: Healthy relationships after childhood trauma (p. 67).

reason to behave in conforming ways so that you can be accepted. This is not what God intended for us. "God has not given us a spirit of fear", but he has given us a "spirit of love" (2 Timothy 1:7). Love is God's reason for anyone to seek connection because you want to experience a godly thing.

Fear can seem like a good reason to be alone because you don't want to be hurt. When you are alone, it means you are safe, and if you are only safe when you're alone, you learn that safety only comes at the price of losing relationships.

Either way, terrible dilemma—be connected (which is human) and feel terrified or be isolated and be safe"[11]. Relationships are supposed to enhance safety and a sense of belonging, not take away safety.

THE SINS OF OUR FATHERS

Our past has a way of finding us in the future. There are certain genetic and cultivated tendencies that we inherit from our parents, and many of them are detrimental to our personal and spiritual growth.

In the springtime, when kings usually go out to war, David stayed behind in Jerusalem (2 Samuel 11:1). While walking

---

[11] Ibid

on the rooftop of his residency, he saw this lady. The bible calls her a very beautiful lady. Mesmerized by her beauty, David sends for her, and when she came, David forced himself on her.

> ***Our past has a way of finding us in the future.***

Similarly, Amnon, David's oldest son, demonstrated his father's behaviour. Amnon had a sister called Tamar, whom the bible coincidentally calls "beautiful," and Amnon loved her (2 Samuel 13:1). So Amnon does what's in the family tree. Through the counsel of his cousin, Jonadab, Amnon comes up with a plan to be alone with Tamar. When they were alone, he forced himself onto her.

The cycle of taking things by force is passed on from generation to generation. "The sins of one generation imprint the next generation. Each sin not only fosters more sin, but it also fashions it by providing precedents for others to follow[12]". You may or may not have a clue about the problems that run in your family. It doesn't really matter.

---

[12] 1, 2 Samuel: An Exegetical and Theological Exposition of Holy Scripture

The reality is, we are forced to contend with an unknown enemy.

Cultivated tendencies can have a significant impact on our success relationally. Before Isaac died, he was supposed to "pronounce the blessing that belong[ed] to *his* firstborn son" (Genesis 27:3). In preparation for this blessing, Isaac told Esau how to make the appropriate arrangements to receive his blessing. As he was giving Esau the instructions, Rebekah was eavesdropping on the conversation.

With an elaborate plan, Rebekah persuaded Jacob to go ahead of Esau. The plan was to have Jacob deceive his father into giving him the blessing which belonged to his brother Esau. Jacob's name means *deceiver*, but that was not all him (nature). Some of it was linked to his mother Rebekah (nurture). Jacob's deceitful collaboration with his mother to steal the birthright from Esau, succeeded. "From that time on, Esau hated Jacob...and Esau vowed to kill Jacob after their father's death" (Genesis 27:41).

The potential to be emotionally mature and loving siblings was lost. Fear took the place of love, and Rebekah their mother, planted the seed of sibling favouritism.

When Jacob becomes of age to marry, he is tricked by his father-in-law, and ends up taking two sisters as his wives. The younger sister initially struggles to have children of her own, and finally, she does; Joseph and Benjamin. These are the last two sons of 12. These two sons, Joseph and Benjamin, are from Jacob's favourite wife, Rachel. Now, "Jacob loved Joseph more than any of his other children." There it is again, the spirit of favouritism.

The story goes, "one day Jacob had a special gift made for Joseph—a beautiful robe" (Genesis 37:3, NLT). This caused strife with the other brothers "because their father loved him more than the rest of them…they couldn't say a kind word to him" (Genesis 37:4). The same divisive spirit that he got from his mother still existed. Jacob was well trained in the dysfunctional ways of his parents.

Ever wonder why you like to gossip?

Why you have such a lying tongue?

Why your eye always wonders after every man or woman that pass by?

Why you have failed to tame your anger?

When your temper rises, no one can stay around you. No matter what you do and how you invest in relationships, they seem to fall apart. Your intention is never to break any relationship, but it just happens. An unhealthy lifestyle and poor financial habits have become the norm.

Shame, secrets, lies, betrayals, relationship breakdowns, disappointments, and unresolved longings for unconditional love lie beneath the veneer of even the most respectable families. We are a broken people. And we carry that brokenness to the next relationship and the next, building a legacy of scars and pain.

Maybe you need to look up your family tree. There might be a beast in you, fighting the beauty that God wants to manifest in you. There is lost potential that is waiting to be found.

> *Christ-centred relationships are centred on understanding intergenerational curses and blessings that plague our families.*

Christ-centred relationships are centred on understanding intergenerational curses and blessings that plague our families. When we get to that aha moment, we can then realize, *it was lost potential, but now it is found*. The cycle can be broken.

CHECK-IN

Each time I travel away from home, I have a hard time packing. All the things that I want to put in my baggage doesn't always seem to fit.

Checked baggage has limitations. Because of the limitations, you are forced to leave stuff behind. But if you want to proceed with everything, you have to pay the price.

It pains me when l leave something at home and get to my destination only to realize, that shirt would have been good for this occasion now. Sometimes, I might even pay extra for it, and I'm fine with that. It might slow me down as I navigate from destination to destination, and that's ok.

Nowadays, it seems like it's ok to have baggage, even in excess.

Not only do we carry baggage when we travel, we also carry it in our lives. You have been carrying baggage in your life for so long, and now you think it's ok. It's ok to stay angry because of what they did to you. You think it's ok not to forgive because you will be perceived as weak.

Baggage from your past relationships, has the tendency to keep manifesting itself in unhealthy ways.

You have been abused and undervalued. Now you think all men or women are the same.

Baggage causes you to view all your relationships through the lens of your brokenness.

The prodigal son was carrying baggage that left him scrabbling for a job and eventually "sent him into his fields to feed the pigs" (Luke 15:15). And when he "came to his senses, he said to himself, 'at home, the hired servants have food enough to spare, and here I am dying of hunger" (Luke 15:17). That was a moment of realization that there was lost potential between him and his family. He began to grieve the time that had been stolen from him. There was a realization that *I am worth much more than I have come to believe about myself.*

When he got back to his father's house, his father embraced him, put a ring on his finger, and gave him a robe to cover himself. You will not realize what God wants to put on you until you lay down your baggage.

> ***You will not realize what God wants to put on you until you lay down your baggage.***

Check-in your baggage with God, he is a baggage keeper. You don't have to go through life regretting your past. God can help you redeem the years that have been lost.

GROW!

1. What has been limiting you from realizing your potential?
2. Have you discovered your purpose?
3. Whose image have you adopted as your own?

BLURRED BOUNDARIES

"Blurred boundaries in relationships cause role ambiguity and relational stress."

GOD SET IT THIS WAY

Before I had any children, I would often hear parents tell their children to say hello to people they engage in conversation. While the poor child clings onto the parent's leg, the parent continues to nudge the child, telling them to say "hi."

Quite frankly, I think feeling a little bit rejected by the child, they try to entice the child. Maybe by pulling out a piece of candy or something to try and win the child's affection. To no avail, the child leaves with the parent without extending their hand.

There were countless times when I saw this happen but missed something in this interaction. In fact, I never thought much about this until I had my own children.

I have observed my shy 3-year-old daughter refuse to greet some people on occasion. It had never dawned on me that she was setting boundaries.

It was clear in her mind that I don't know you, and you are trying to be friendly and nice, but it's scaring me.

Setting boundaries is a trait that we are all born with.

Babies learn and become familiar with their parent's heartbeat before they even recognize their faces. They soon learn to attach to their family and refuse to be left with someone they don't recognize.

This is not only a phenomenon common to babies, but it also extends to everywhere in life.

Boundaries are everywhere, visible and invisible.

You might be familiar with fences and walls that we use to mark property lines and keep away intruders.

The Wi-Fi you have in your home has built-in boundaries that have been reinforced with a password accessible only to friends and family.

To the seas, God said, "This far and no farther will you come. Here your proud waves must stop!" (Job 38:11).

Signs for male and female accessibility are everywhere. If you remove boundaries or blur the lines, dysfunction is inevitable.

Boundaries are a healthy part of normal life.

From the earliest times, humanity has been involved with God, in a relationship with defined boundaries. God set them as he created heaven and Earth. "God placed the man in the Garden of Eden to tend and watch over it" (Genesis 2:15). After placing him in this beautiful Garden, God set the first boundary for mankind. "From any tree of the garden, you may eat freely; but from the tree of the knowledge of good and evil you shall not eat".

If you remove boundaries or blur the lines, dysfunction is inevitable.

Adam and Eve had full dominion and could eat from all the trees except one. Of that one, God said, "Don't eat of it, it's reserved for me." Not only were they not to eat it, but consequences were also set for disobeying, "for in the day that you eat from it, you will surely die" (Genesis 2:15-17).

The tree of good and evil was a visible and tangible way of demonstrating their allegiance, trust, and dependence upon God.

Setting boundaries is a principle given by God.

THE FALLACY OF BOUNDARIES

What was the most awkward moment you have ever had?

Was it with a coworker? Maybe you saw them secretly taking some office supplies for personal use at home.

Was it at church? Maybe someone told a lie and asked you to go along.

Was it an uncomfortable random text message that came in quite late at night? Maybe it's a married person.

Was it your best friend's unfaithfulness, and you were supposed to be cool with it and back them up in case there's a fall out?

At some point in your life, you've had some blurred lines that created some awkward moments. When you accommodate dysfunctional behaviour, you create an inroad to undermining your dignity. One conversation at a time, one encounter at a time, you begin to normalize people moving into your personal space.

There are several misconceptions about boundaries that people have come to embrace. This often arises from normalized behaviours and scars that have developed over time and have become deeply ingrained.

The following are four common views that people hold about boundaries:

The price you will pay for confronting the issue is greater than dismissing it. Of the many, the main misconception that people have come to embrace consciously and subconsciously, is the thinking that I'm uncomfortable now, but it will be better later.

There is the delusion that time is a healer. When we give time to any issue, it will settle itself out.

This is an erroneous thought that arises from the confusion between time and timing. Everything must have the right timing in order to address it adequately. But no issue will be resolved by letting time lapse. The scars won't heal; they just develop scar tissue that makes it difficult to heal later. The issue will also be and will often be triggered by similar situations as the original.

When Adam and Eve ate from the tree that they were not supposed to touch, "God banished them from the Garden of Eden...After sending them out, he put an angel *with* a flaming sword... to guard the way to the tree of life (Genesis 3:23-24).

It pained God to be separated from His creation, but the cost of ignoring the issue was greater than confronting it. Sin could not be ignored. But that was not God's last attempt to restore his relationship with mankind.

Loss of boundaries is the price you have pay in order to belong. Losing yourself is not an acceptable price to pay for the connection. Once you make that negotiable, you will continue to pay the price of having your opinions and desires to be made invisible. This is all at the cost of keeping something that looks like a connection, but instead, it is a toxic relationship.

Don't violate your boundaries at the cost of losing yourself. You don't have to give up your values, your voice, and your safety in order to belong in any relationship.

You don't have to give up your values, your voice, and your safety in order to belong in any relationship..

Adam and Eve enjoyed face to face communion with God. After they had eaten the forbidden fruit from the tree of good and evil, their relationship with God wasn't the same anymore. Once again, "They heard the sound of the LORD God as he was walking in the garden in the cool of the day" coming to commune with them (Genesis 3:8). But this time, something changed, Adam and Eve "hid from" God.

The relationship between God and our first parents was broken because they had disobeyed God. They hid from God because they thought they had to pay a price to belong. Though God loved them, he did not ignore their disobedience. Sin has consequences.

The value system that governed their relationship was not ignored. Their acceptance as children of God was not contingent on their behaviour.

The healthy relationship was not lost; but they still belonged to God. God made a promise to restore them. Through the victory on the cross, "He will strike your head, and you will strike his heel" (Genesis 3:15). No boundaries were lost for Adam and Eve to belong to God.

Ignoring something you didn't like is a way of dismissing the issue. The derogatory comments that you have ignored for the sake of keeping the peace are unhealthy boundaries. Ignoring things that you don't like creates a pathway for them to be repeated because you have not declared your position on the issue.

Imagine the awkward silence that gripped the air when God asked Adam and Eve, "who told you that you were naked?" (Genesis 3:11). God didn't dismiss the issue because he loved them, but instead, he addressed it by telling them what they had done wrong.

Ignoring something you don't like only empowers the offender to do it again because the precedence indicated it was ok the last time.

You may feel like the issue will work itself out, but instead, it just strains your relationships more because there's an elephant in the room. Ignoring something you don't like only empowers the offender to do it again because the precedence indicated it was ok the last time.

Ignorance is excusable. Just because someone didn't know, it does not make it "ok" for them to go beyond their limitations.

There is a tendency to absolve people of their guilt because they had no idea that you didn't like it. Adam certainly thought so, "the woman you put here with me--she gave me some fruit from the tree, and I ate it" (Genesis 3:12). Eve did get her reproach from God. And to Adam God said, "The ground is cursed because of you. All your life you will struggle to scratch a living from it" (Genesis 3:17). He was not absolved of his sin.

Ignorance is not an excuse to absolve people from moving into your personal space. The conversation still needs to happen. Practice creating boundaries by saying, "I don't like what you did".

Healthy boundaries don't always come naturally. We may learn healthy and unhealthy boundaries all at the same time. While some are learned, others are developed through experiences along life's journey. People that have been emotionally, spiritually, and physically abused in the past, tend to have unhealthy boundaries because they have come to believe many fallacies about boundaries.

Their normal has been defined by abnormal situations. There are many things about boundaries that we've come to embrace as good but beneath the quest for healthy interpersonal relationships lies dysfunctional habits that undermine our desires. What we allow to define us, determines our future.

> *What we allow to define us, determines our future.*

SETTING BOUNDARIES

When you decide you want to set boundaries, you will receive a lot of pushback. People might feel like you've been deceitful and dishonest about your actual feelings.

Who changes the rules of the game in the relationship midway?

Quite frankly, you might feel like you've betrayed people's trust, and you may even fall for the trap of thinking this is a bad idea. But that's to be expected.

It can be quite daunting to tell your best friend that you don't want to anymore.

Your employer may think you are getting an attitude.

Your relationship might see some rough times, just because you decided to get real. It won't be unusual for you to have your boundaries questioned. In some cases, you might experience guilt-or-shame-statements. Guilt and shame are just invitations to let go of your boundaries. You might even take some of these trips into guilt or shame as you begin setting boundaries.

So, here's the question, how do you learn to set boundaries?

Begin with the simplest and the most powerful of things—your five senses.

Your five senses tend to be an accurate indicator of what you like and don't like. When you look at something you don't like, you cringe. If there's a strong nasty smell, your face will show disgust, and if it's sweet, your face will show delight. Boundary setting is your response to your five senses. Resist the urge to think about what would make the other person happy. There is a time and place for that.

Right now, you want to build a fence that has been broken down.Resist beginning with,

"what will make someone like me?"

"What would my parents want me to do?"

The key to developing healthy boundaries is self-awareness[13]. Self-awareness starts with seemingly simple things: touch, taste, smell, colour, sound—Your five senses! Rediscover yourself.

What do you like?

As you grow in knowing yourself, you will exercise the "power of choice" muscle easier.

RELATIONSHIP MARKERS

It's a nice thought to think that relationships have to be flexible, allowing for gray areas to become clear as we go along. However, that can be a recipe for disaster.

An undefined relationship status can cause role ambiguity. This may be with your friends, professional acquaintances, and intimate partners. Simply put, there has to be a clear distinction on where the line is drawn on things that are acceptable and unacceptable in the relationship. And when people don't know what they can or can't do, misunderstandings are bound to happen.

It's crucial for every relationship to embrace relationship markers. Relationship markers are principles that you can use

---

[13] Brown, Laura S. Not the price of admission: Healthy relationships after childhood trauma (p. 88).

to dispel role ambiguity and avoid toxic relationships while enhancing the relationship.

Adam and Eve were created outside of Eden. God planted a garden "in Eden; and there He placed the man whom he had formed" (Genesis 2:8). In the "Garden of Eden" God put two things that would serve as relationship markers; the tree of the 'knowledge of good and evil', and the "seventh day".

The tree and the seventh day were markers that were meant to enhance Adam and Eve's relationship with God.

The Garden of Eden was a marked boundary.

The tree and the seventh day were markers that were meant to enhance Adam and Eve's relationship with God. The lines were evident in the relationship because of the markers that were set by God.

The boundaries you set for yourself and your relationships can serve to enhance your relationships in several ways:

As a form of clarifying a relationship—relationship markers help you develop self-awareness. They define what kind of relationship should exist between you and others, what you are and what you are not.

Placing the tree in the Garden of Eden defined and clarified the kind of relationship the couple would have with God. And in turn, it also defined the kind of relationship they had with each other. The instruction was given to Adam, "any tree of the garden you may eat freely; but [not] from the tree of the knowledge of good and evil" (Genesis 2:16). Eve was not there, and when Eve was created, Adam bore the responsibility of providing her God's instruction about the tree. The tree was a marker of their relationship with God.

The tree also served as a visible symbol of a covenantal agreement between God, and Adam and Eve.

The covenant was governed by free will, the freedom to choose to accept God's proposal or reject it. Adam and Eve were to exercise their free will, their love for God was not coerced. In seeing how God loved them, and had given them free will of choice, they too were to exercise the same love one to another.

As a form of confrontation—relationship markers help you discern places and relationships you should belong to. The markers that people place indicate exclusion or inclusion, where you end and where you begin.

From the tree of the knowledge of good and evil you shall not eat, for in the day that you eat from it you will surely die" (Genesis 2:17). The tree indicated how they were to relate to each other, and where their jurisdiction started and ended. It is a way of delineating common and personal space.

A person with clear, healthy boundaries communicates to others what is and is not permissible, saying, in effect, "This is my jurisdiction, my space, and you have no right to interfere." If I do let you in, you can only come this far. Anything beyond what I have allowed you to come will have consequences.

Adam and Even certainly knew and understood all of this. A confrontation is not necessarily a bad thing, it is a safety measure in place to ensure the relationship bliss is protected.

You may be on the receiving end, where boundaries are set against you. And when you are, learn to deal with it in a healthy manner by respecting where you are wanted and not wanted. Not only deal with it in a healthy manner but move on from it. When you know who you are and your place, it allows you to "anticipate and deal with [boundary shifts] in a healthy manner"[14]. Nothing catches you off guard.

As a form of connection—relationship markers can help intimacy grow by creating time to cultivate mutual respect and trust. Boundaries pave the way for understanding each other intimately.

---

[14] Brown, Laura S. Not the price of admission: Healthy relationships after childhood trauma (p. 213).

The last crowning act of God's creation was on the sixth day when God created mankind. On the seventh day God rested, inviting mankind to join Him in a completed work, where He "blessed the Seventh day and sanctified it" (Genesis 2:3). God set a boundary on time to create space for intimacy.

Without investing time in a relationship, all the self-sacrifice and being nice will not make any deposits in your emotional bank account

The first thing that Adam and Eve experienced with one another and with God was quality time. When you set aside sacred time for things you want to invest in, you create opportunities for intimacy to grow.

Without investing time, all the self-sacrifice and being nice will not make any deposits in your emotional bank account. You won't guarantee yourself a healthy connection without spending time being transparent and open, and both of these qualities come over time.

Carving out sacred time for your relationships will allow you to form stronger connections, creating greater closeness. It allows everyone to realize that they are worth more and are loveable.

A skewed sense of self-worth is the enemy of intimacy because it overlooks the fact that we are loved by God and therefore we are loveable.

HOW NOT TO BUY LOVE

Boundaries help us understand that we have value and personal worth with others because God has determined our worth first. A worth that gives a realization that there is no one else like me, I am needed in the family of God, and so I am valuable to God and others. This is how the "Father loves us, and he calls us his children, and that is what we are!" (1 John 3:1 NLT).

Your perception of value to God and others is based on how you see God as loving and forgiving.

Understanding your value and worth allows you to see that we can be different and still value and accept each other for our differences.

Love was never meant to be a wage that you receive after having worked yourself to emotional bankruptcy. You can certainly work to make a relationship flourish, but it should never be taxing to be in a relationship where you are loved and valued.

How Not to Buy Love

First, realize that your worth is derived from God, not from those that are around you. Once you come to understand that, you have the right to say yes and no to what you like and don't like. Low self-esteem undermines God's creative power. You were made in the image of God, and no failure can devalue your worth. Failure will only come in as far as you allow it to take residence in your thoughts. If you don't define your boundaries, other people will define them for you.

Second, you are not chained to your past. There are no incidents that are isolated. Everything soon becomes a common thread in your relationships. Before you realize it, everyone who comes into your life becomes an opportunity to re-enact painful patterns of people that you've let in too far beyond the point you desired.

> *Life is a journey, and each footprint is just as much of the beginning as the final destination.*

Only when you stop seeing yourself and others through the lens of your past, are you able to then begin to build confidence to set healthy boundaries. People do not decide their futures. They decide their habits and their habits decide their futures[15]. Life is a journey, and each footprint is just as much of the beginning as the final destination.

When the San Francisco Bay Golden Gate Bridge was being built, construction fell badly behind schedule. Several workers had accidentally fallen from the scaffolding to their deaths.

Engineers and administrators could find no solution to costly delays.

Finally, someone suggested a gigantic net be hung under the bridge to catch anyone who fell.

The idea was absurd, but there was no other option. Despite the enormous cost, the engineers opted for the net. All who fell short towards their death were caught by the net. Ultimately, all the time lost to fear was regained by replacing fear with faith in the net.

Boundaries can be your safety net how not to buy love. They can help revive the self-worth that has been lost. Build self-worth and self-esteem that has been eroded by many years of lost boundaries.

---

[15] F. M. Alexander

GROW!

You can check how healthy your boundaries are by asking the following questions:

1. Do you find it easy to tell people the things you don't like?

2. Do you find it better to let it go than to be confrontational?

3. When people talk about things they have achieved, do you feel the need to demonstrate your worth by sharing your accomplishments?

6

EMOTIONAL MATURITY

"Relational success is an integral part of emotional maturity."

I AM AN EMOTINAL BEING

In 2015, the Oxford Dictionary Word of the Year was a laughing emoji. Can you imagine that? This word was used such a significant number of times to warrant its consideration for Word of the Year. Over the course of 12 months, several words are considered for the Word of the Year title. In 2015, it was apparent that emotions had been overlooked until an emoji with the expression came along.

Isn't it true that we often don't give good credit to our emotions, yet they are the most influential aspect of our decision making? We often say don't trust your emotions; and those who have attended to them, have received much criticism.

Our capitalist society has mastered the human psyche well. Products are marketed with the intention to evoke a certain emotional response. The right colours coupled with the right images ingeniously blended can make quite a profit.

I will admit, emotions often get us into trouble.

Follow them at your own risk.

Many of the scars that people carry come from a pursuit that was initiated by a feeling. It's not that you wanted to act that way; you were just caught off guard by anger. And before you knew it, you were in conflict, and unforgiveness followed. The slope was just too slippery. It is a downward spiral to brokenness. You didn't mean to, but one thing led to another.

THE HEART

Our hearts can often lead us in the wrong path, which is, of course, the evidence of sin. "The human heart is the most deceitful…and desperately wicked (Jeremiah 17:9, NLT). But have you ever considered that God might be reaching out to you through your "emotions" in a way that did not compromise the truth?

We often make the statements, "I just made an emotional decision" or "You can never trust your heart." However, what if God was reaching out and we have been dismissing him because we've declared that we can't trust emotions?

One of the most recited Hebrew prayers is the Shema, "Hear, O Israel! The LORD is our God, the LORD is one! You shall love the LORD your God with all your heart and with all your soul and with all your might" (Deuteronomy 6:4-5). It was recited twice a day, in the morning and evening. Every child was to be taught this prayer as soon as they could start speaking.

Families were to speak about it in every home, when they sat, walked, lay down, and arose. In everything they did, they had to breathe the Shema. It was fundamental to their existence and relationship to God.

One word stands out in that prayer, "heart." Love God with your heart. The heart in a Hebraic mind didn't mean what we have come to understand now. They spoke of the heart in some ways that may seem strange to the reader now.

In the bible, you know and understand with your heart. It is where you think and make sense of the world.

Certainly, in the book of Proverbs, wisdom enters and dwells in your heart (Proverbs 2:10).

You discern truth and error from the heart like Solomon did when he was a King (1 Kings 3:9).

There was no concept of brain function, so all the brain activity and more was transferred to the heart.

It was also considered the seat of your emotions.

You feel joy in your heart (Judges 16:25).

The evidence of the love of God at work in us is the joy that we experience. The experience of fear and distress comes from the heart.

The birth of the Prophet Samuel is a classic example. The annual pilgrimage to Shiloh for sacrifice was the most dreaded time for Hannah. Peninnah would rub it in her face that she couldn't have children. Her loving husband Elkanah would ask, "Hannah, why do you weep? Why do you not eat? And why is your heart grieved?" (1 Samuel 1:8, NKJV).

Her emotions were stirred up. She was in emotional pain; she had a broken heart. But also, when she went to the temple to pray, she did not pray out loud, she "spoke in her heart; only her lips moved, but her voice was not heard" (1 Samuel 1:13, NKJV).

Her mental capacities were being engaged. The same word, heart, is used in at least two different ways.

The heart in the Hebrew thought is understood as the seat that controls thought and intellect. At the same time, emotional life flowed from the heart with choices motivated by your desires. I know that's a mouthful.

Simply put, the heart was responsible for your whole being in understanding and experiencing God intimately.

In an exchange with one of the Pharisees, Jesus affirms their response to receive eternal life you must "love the LORD your God with all your heart" (Luke 10:27). This was the total response of love towards God, including your emotions.

God is interested in this part of you that we've relegated to negative outcomes.

God wants you to seek him, "with all my heart" (Psalm 119:10). He speaks to our whole being and desires to transform you whole.

If your emotional being has not been surrendered to God, He can't lead you into relational satisfaction.

God created you as an emotional and rational being. All areas of your life belong to him.

> *If your emotional being has not been surrendered to God, He can't lead you into relational satisfaction.*

You are to "delight yourself in the LORD, and he will give you the desires of your heart" (Psalm 37:4). God can speak to you through your emotions in ways that do not compromise biblical integrity.

I ONCE WAS YOUNG

Everything that affects our relationships is deeply rooted in our emotional response.

How do you handle your emotions when unsettling events show up in your life?

When you are betrayed, how do you navigate life after that?

Every person needs to understand their emotions and how they affect them and others around them. As you grow physiologically, you must be growing emotionally too. Physical maturity is easy to notice and measure. However, it's not always easy to see how you are growing emotionally.

Everything that affects our relationships is deeply rooted in our emotional response.

Emotional maturity is the ability to identify and manage your own emotions and respond to the emotions of others in a healthy manner[16]. Instead of blaming the issue on someone, you seek to fix the issue. The problem is usually never the

---

[16] Marilyn McMahon

person, and the problem can be identified and separated from the person.

Emotional maturity is knowing how to communicate effectively without being overtaken by feelings.

Integral to emotional maturity is self-awareness. You are most vulnerable when you love. When you are in a state of loving, you open up and let your guard down. All past pains, fears, and heartaches that had been buried begin to surface.

Think about it for a moment, who can hurt you the most?

It's people that we love, people whom you have given over your trust entirely. Our family, friends, and intimate partners can hurt us the most. This might not be their intention, but love is something you learn, it can be taught right and wrong. Giving "good" does not mean that it will be reciprocated. When you get into a relationship without an awareness of who you are emotionally, you become exposed to hurt and pain.

Love can reveal old wounds that have never healed. Even as you allow yourself to entertain the wish that this time love might heal you, it never does. You can also be abusive in your language and actions without even knowing it because you never healed. "Wounds heal from the inside out and the bottom up.

They must be kept open, inspected, [and] known[17]. That is part of the process of maturing emotionally.

When you are not aware of your emotional disposition, you might feel like you always have to pay the price to belong in some relationships. There is always this price for admission that never gets paid in full. Like a customer on a month-to-month agreement with a cell phone provider who will never tell you the grounds for service termination, until you no longer see text messages and calls come through.

Changes in relationship closeness will always feel like another loss is waiting to happen. A setup for disappointment to take place. But in reality, it is nothing other than life happening.

When you learn to respond to your emotions in healthy and meaningful ways, you are well on your way to emotional maturity. Relationships become a relational exchange, not an informational exchange where transactions characterize your connection. A healthy relationship where two emotionally mature individuals enjoy connection is characterized by a past that does not show up unannounced. There is vulnerability enjoyed mutually at no risk.

---

[17] ProActive ReSolutions. (n.d.). 5 Steps to Managing Emotions At Work. Retrieved November 16, 2019, from https://proactive-resolutions.com/article/managing-your-emotions-at-work-2/.

EMOTIONAL ICEBERG

Emotionally broken people are unpredictable to others and themselves. Very few people emerge out of their families of origin emotionally whole and mature[18]. Whenever a negative or positive reaction is triggered, what we see in people is the behavioural and physiological response.

Behavioural response is how you voluntarily act in response to a situation. This may be clapping your hands to cheer or giving someone a joyful hug. These are all responses we see or visualize people doing.

On the other hand, physiological responses are how the body responds to situations, like perspiration, crying, or shaking. It is how your body involuntarily responds physically to any situation.

Behavioural and physiological responses are based on people's past experiences in similar situations. The body becomes conditioned to respond in a similar way when it senses it's being put in a familiar experience.

If a child who has been abused sees an adult raising their hand, the immediate reaction is to hide their head. It might

---

[18] Scazzero, Peter. Emotionally Healthy Spirituality (p. 9). Zondervan.

be that the raised hand had nothing to do with hitting the child, but their response is based on past similar situations.

It happens in relationships as well. Family and friends might comment on a presentation you did. If you think the criticism is negative, it might trigger a sense of low self-esteem and sense of worth. Because in the past, you were told you would never amount to nothing, so these comments become a reminder of your past.

Primarily, what we pay attention to in any relationship, is the behavioural response, which is the symptom not the cause. Just like an iceberg, underneath the surface of any response and reaction, there is a motivating factor.

The emotional response is usually the motivating factor of the physiological and behavioural responses; fear, shame, and anxiety. Some people might be rude because they have experienced abuse in the past, and they feel they have to protect themselves. You can't look at a person and say definitively what they feel. But you can identify the behavioural and physiological responses associated with the emotions.

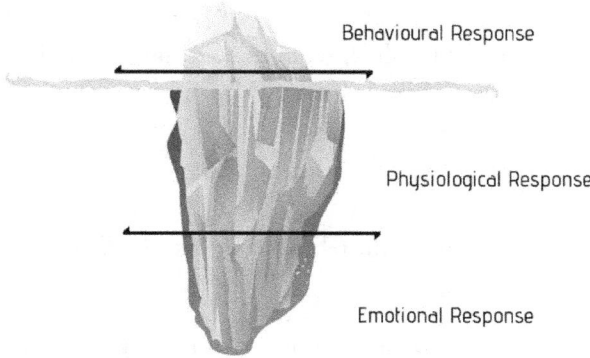

Typical of any iceberg, there's always more to the story. What you see is not the whole story. The behaviour may be due to factors that lie underneath; insecurity, trauma, envy, anger, etc. It might be a deep longing for attention but failing to communicate it in healthy ways.

Relationships suffer because we don't have the whole puzzle to piece the pieces together and understand each other.

Some relationships suffer because healing has not occurred yet from a past experience, and you are still bleeding from past wounds. And if you are not honest with yourself to confront what lies beneath the iceberg, you will not heal. It is important to be patient with people and try to understand their story.

Being able to have emotionally-meaningful relationships with other people is a skill which requires continuous practice.

EMOTINAL MATURITY AND SPIRITUALITY

Awareness of self and your relationship with God are intricately intertwined.

When surrendered to God, emotions can be a godly thing. He created us as emotional beings. Relationships thrive when there is self-awareness of your emotional disposition by nurture and nature. How you manage your emotions is an important aspect of how you grow spiritually.

> *Awareness of self and your relationship with God are intricately intertwined*

"Christian spirituality, without an integration of emotional health, can be deadly—to yourself, your relationship with God, and the people around you"[19]. When things are said about you, they don't have to define you.

---

[19] Ibid.

Emotional maturity is directly related to spiritual maturity. The way we relate to each other reveals Christ when our emotions are under control.

King Saul had delayed emotional growth, which became evident in his spiritual response. He eventually started working for God, but not with God. At 30 years old when he was crowned King, literally he had his head above the shoulders, "a choice and handsome *man*" (1 Samuel 9:2). At the onset of his reign, he was set to thrive under the guidance of the prophet Samuel.

God picked Saul out, he was the first choice King to rule over his people and he realized success in most of his military conquests. God's guiding hand was always over Saul. Something changed with Saul along the way. He started making a series of strange decisions.

The Philistines remained a constant threat to the Israelites. And before Israel went to battle, they would offer sacrifices and consult God on a course of action. Saul summoned the people to rally for battle against the Philistines. And while they waited for Samuel the Priest to come and do the sacrifice, he never showed up. Saul fearing that the people were beginning to scatter from him, he said, "Bring to me the burnt offering and the peace offerings. And he offered the burnt offering" (1 Samuel 13:9). Only the priest is supposed to offer sacrifices, but Saul had some insecurities. His irrational temperament was tied to his spirituality and trust in God.

Again, while encamped in the battlefield with hungry and thirsty soldiers, Saul issued a command, "cursed be the man who eats food before evening, and until I have avenged myself on my enemies" (1 Samuel 13:24).

This was strange because troops need to eat and be at their optimal strength. It happens the only person who disobeyed the command was the crowned, Prince Jonathan. Saul was determined to execute his judgment, "for you shall surely die, Jonathan" ... the people rescued Jonathan and he did not die (1 Samuel 13:44-45). Saul had become irrational and impatient, and his decisions became increasingly selfish.

When Saul saw any mighty or valiant man, he attached them to his staff. (1 Samuel 14:52). Saul sought to compensate for his low self-esteem and insecurity by getting great warriors by his side.

His fate was sealed when God wanted to Judge "Amalek *for* what he did to Israel", so, He told King Saul to "go and completely destroy the entire Amalekite nation" (1 Samuel 15:3). This was no strange request. Saul was a representative of God's sovereignty on Earth. He wasn't God but he was God's agent to the people. Saul went and did as instructed but he "took *some* of the spoil, sheep and oxen, the choicest...to sacrifice to the Lord" (1 Samuel 15:3). He disobeyed God in trying to please God. Saul was working for God, but not with God. His spirituality was directly linked to his temperament.

Once again, when David, a great warrior, came on Saul's radar, David was supposed to be Saul's greatest ally but became his greatest enemy. Twice, Saul tried to pin him to the wall with a spear.

The people celebrated and hailed David as the hero of the Israelites and composed melodies over his victories. All this enraged King Saul, he hated David so much that he would have him marry his daughter to keep him close. He even tried to get him killed by asking for a bride price of Philistine foreskins (1 Samuel 18:25). Now, that's a demented King who has lost it emotionally and spiritually.

What might have been going on beneath the surface (iceberg) of Saul's life?

He had so much insecurity.

Fear compelled him not to trust even his allies.

He used his daughters as pawns in his plot to destroy David.

He was rejected by God as King, and that became his trigger downwards to the abyss of his demise.

It's easy to confuse spiritual experiences—such as worship, prayer, and Bible studies as an indicator that you are spiritually fine. While they may be good practices of faith, they are not indicators of good spiritual health. Anger, anxiety, and fear might be still pulling you back from experiencing God's worth. Some Christians are characterized by a lack of emotional regulation, an inability to regulate how one responds to their inclinations. A good indicator of emotional immaturity is how often you express your feelings inappropriately.

Without an integration of emotional health, your spirituality may be stuck in falseness and an empty pursuit of performance. Which in essence is trying to earn God's grace.

> *Without an integration of emotional health, your spirituality may be stuck in falseness and an empty pursuit of performance.*

When you grow spiritually, you should grow emotionally. A disruption of this flow is counterproductive to your maturity as a Christian.

THE MIND OF CHRIST

When Christ walked on earth, he had a host of emotions (joy, pain, love, anger, etc.) that he had to contend with in order to have a good relationship with God and men. Christ had all of his emotions under control by the guidance of the Holy Spirit.

The Pharisees called him names and spat on him.

Satan tried to offer Christ his Kingdom as if it didn't belong to Christ.

He was beaten to get him to confess that he is not the Son of God.

All in all, he maintained composure. Christ's conduct gave a revelation of the character of God. He was the perfect example of an emotionally balanced being, given wholly to God, and trusting God.

Sometimes our emotions are grounded in "falsehood," not "truth". When you believe that God is not in control of the circumstances of your lives, you may experience the emotions of fear, despair, and anger.

We fail to trust God in all our circumstances. God set the example so that you too might "let this mind be in you which was in Christ Jesus" (Philippians 2:5, NKJV). In whatever circumstances my emotions are triggered, God must be glorified. In my joy and in sadness, all in all, Jesus gave a testimony of his God. Jesus trusted his father wholly and submitted everything to him.

The brain is an interesting phenomenon. Brain research has revealed that when we engage in an activity, there are certain brain pathways that are created. When you engage in toxic emotional habits, you begin to normalize things that are toxic, and these brain pathways are strengthened. However, these brain pathways that are associated with being emotional can be transformed over time from their previously well-worn grooves. These new pathways, like any young thing, will be more fragile, but will tend to develop into healthy pathways for loving others, like God desires to love us.

God can create a new path in your life and recalibrate your emotional compass.

> ***God can create a new path in your life and recalibrate your emotional compass.***

All you need is to surrender like Jesus. Let the mind of Christ be in you.

GROW!

1. Are you reactive instead of responsive to emotional stressors in your life?
2. Are you making requests to God without surrendering your will to him?
3. Do you measure your spirituality by the number of bible studies you have, the number of sermons you watch, and how often you attend church? Or by the relational quality you have with God and people around you?

KINGSLEY MOYO

7

INTEGRITY

"Integrity is the first sacrifice on the altar of reconciliation."

WHO IS GOING TO BE NUMBER 1?

In 2003, there was a global SARS outbreak, a respiratory disease that claimed the lives of its victim by causing a difficulty in breathing. The effects of the deadly disease were felt throughout Canada, and most notably in Ontario.

When the outbreak was officially declared, there was a province wide panic. Precautionary measures were outlined and advised. It was highly emphasized to wash your hands or sanitize them in the absence of water. Demand for hand sanitizer grew significantly, but supplies were low. The law of supply and demand dictates that when demand is high and supply is low, cost must inevitably increase.

Amidst all this, some hand sanitizer brands took the opportunity to hike sales upwards to 160%. Purell, a household brand, took center stage because they never increased their prices at any point during the outbreak.

For the past 10 consecutive years, Purell had been losing money. Any business strategist would have advised the company to seize the moment, hike prices, and boost sales. Not to do so would be foolery.

For Purell, it was an integrity issue. Beyond being loyal to their customers, Purell wanted to win the right way, despite their circumstances.

Every relationship is faced with the challenge of who gets to win. We are always competing for time, attention, and affection. Competing is not a problem particular to a certain type of relationship, it exists in all types of relationships.

The first instinct and desire of everyone is to be put first. Subconsciously, everyone looks out for number one. How are my needs being met is a regular feature on the mind? When number one is not being attended to, many respond by losing their integrity.

Integrity is doing the right thing even when no one is watching. Doing the right thing is to love and respect, even when I am hurt and know I am right. We often think of integrity as an individual thing and not as relational. Integrity can only exist when there is two or more people.

Think about it, the only way you have integrity is when you can demonstrate to someone that you can govern yourself in a manner acceptable to others. Integrity does not exist in a vacuum. People demonstrate integrity to other people. We reflect integrity when we have morals that don't waiver, and morals only exist if there is a relationship. Having integrity is the key ingredient to building healthy relationships.

IS ANYONE WATCHING?

Our first sacrifice in times of conflict is integrity.

"I lost myself when he started calling me names."

You don't always plan to, but conflict has a way of altering your sense of right and wrong.

When conflict arises we often cease to see each other as people, family and friends—as human beings.

Our first sacrifice in times of conflict is integrity.

Very few people resolve issues in a mature and healthy manner. Most people simply bury the tension and move on. It especially hurts the most and takes the longest to resolve conflict when it's someone you love. You are most vulnerable with people that you love and trust. Our expectations are greatest with our loved ones, and our disappointments match the expectations.

Whenever we are confronted with conflict, there is an unmentioned reality of who will act with integrity. Tension happens ever so frequently—and when it does, will you act with integrity? Will you lose yourself and succumb to looking out for number 1?

After David slew Goliath, he became an instant national hero. His heroic acts were celebrated with song, and with the same song his fugitive years began.

With another narrow escape from Saul and his men, David once again is on the run. The closest place to take refuge was the city of Keilah. The same city that his men protected by fighting "with the Philistines *leading* away their livestock and *striking* them with a great slaughter" (1 Samuel 23:15). But Keilah was going to betray David and his men, had it not been God who warned him not to seek refuge there.

Saul was on his way with 3,000 soldiers, 10 times as much men than David had.

By now, Saul had made several attempts on David's life.

The scorching sun had David and his men in low spirits. Keliah would have been a good hiding place.

Now they wander from place to place until they settled in the wilderness of Engedi. This was just another close call on his life. The conflict between David and Saul had been brewing for some time now, and David has been on the run for years.

As Saul was coming from yet another Philistines conquest, word goes out informing him of David's hiding place. With 3,000 of his elite troops, Saul went out to search for David. On their way, he takes a rest stop in a cave, which happens to be the same cave where David was hiding.

David's men whispered to him. "Today the LORD is telling you, 'I will certainly put your enemy into your power, to do with as you wish" (1 Samuel 24:4).

Remember, David has been on the run from Saul for years.

Certainly, an opportunity like this must be from God.

You only win when you don't lose your integrity

David is the next anointed King, after all.

His men are tired of running, searching for food and shelter in the wilderness. Not to imagine travelling with their families with no place to call home. David slowly moves closer quietly and "cuts off a piece of the hem of Saul's robe" (1 Samuel 24:4). I'm sure that's not what his men had in mind. But David, even in times of conflict, maintained his integrity. He realized that you only win when you don't lose your integrity.

The Hebrew word translated into *"hem"* is *Kanaf.* Kanaf literally means the *wing* of a garment.

David's conscience began to bother him because he had cut off the hem of the King's garment.

Later, after Saul had left the cave and was at a safe distance, David calls out to him.

When Saul looked behind him, David bowed with his face to the ground and prostrated himself (1 Samuel 24:8). David confessed what he had done. After having his enemy in the palm of his hand, David still honoured Saul as his King.

The relationship David had with Saul was not predicated and altered by the circumstances in between them. The condition of David's action towards Saul was not dependent on Saul's behaviour.

David took full responsibility of doing what is right, even if the situation lended itself well to leveraging his upper hand on his enemy.

Saul told David in response to his confession,

"Now I know that you will become King."

Interesting statement—Saul didn't just sober up over an attempt on his life. If anything, it should have made him angrier. He has been searching high and low for him.

What was the meaning of those words?

In the ancient world, one's authority or power rested in the hem of their garments. The hem of a ruler's garment was an extension of one's royal essence.

Remember the woman with the issue of blood for 12 years who "came up behind [Jesus] and touched the fringe of His cloak, and immediately her hemorrhage stopped"? (Luke 8:44). Jesus felt healing power come out of him and being transferred to the woman with the issue of blood. At that moment when he felt the power come out, he stopped the whole procession.

When David cut off the hem of Saul's garment, he understood that he was acting beyond his authority. What he did signified the transfer of kingly authority and power from Saul to David. Although this was the moment to end it all, he understood and pleaded, "The LORD therefore be judge and decide between you and me; and may He see and plead my cause and deliver me from your hand" (1 Samuel 24:15).

When he was offered the opportunity to avenge himself, he chose the way of integrity. And on this, he was resolved to maintain his integrity.

CONFLICT SNOWBALL

When winter comes around, and snow begins to fall, kids love to build a snowman. And it's not just any snow that will build a good snowman. Fluffy or powdery snow won't work. It must be wet, but not too wet.

Only when it's the right kind of wet will it roll up and make a nice snowball. When the snow is perfectly damp, the kids make nice balls, which they simply roll around. Because of the right consistency, it will accumulate and make a nice big ball for their snowman.

Conflict is like that; it has the tendency of accumulating into a big mess.

Conflict—is the different ways people relate to each other beyond their level of tolerance.

Not all ways of relating to each other are bad, but they can certainly affect our relationships if we ignore them.

Conflict is not a set of isolated incidents. It's a string of incidents that accumulate over time, shaping the way you think and respond to similar situations.

Conflict acts like a snowball. Every part of the snowflakes is crucial to make a huge complete snowman. Correcting one conflict incident does not resolve the dysfunctional mind map of dealing with other issues in your life.

> *Conflict is not a set of isolated incidents. It's a string of incidents that accumulate over time, shaping the way you think and respond to similar situations*

People decide their habits, and their habits determine their futures.

Most people deal with conflict the same way in every relationship. And it all starts with one relationship and spills over to the other. However, the way your family of origin dealt with issues will be the standard for years to come until the cycle is broken. Your family of origin sets the base of how you will continue to deal with conflict everywhere in your life.

You might think you deal with conflict differently with your family than you do with co-workers, but that's rarely the case. In each and every case, conflict manifests itself in different ways.

You might tend to be quiet out of respect when you are at home, and at work it manifests as ignoring the situation to avoid conflict. In both cases, you might just be afraid to express yourself.

A conflict snowball can be very dangerous because it's an accumulation of baggage in all areas of your life. It's the unhealthy way you deal with your siblings, all the way to how you relate to your neighbour. Somewhere in-between are people you have hurt but didn't know because you were carrying a lot of baggage.

People that are closest to you tend to feel it the most. And before you realize it, you have become a difficult person to work with because of the weight that is pulling you down from achieving your potential. The day you can't contain your anger and frustration, you will have a nervous breakdown or an outburst that might make things worse. This is just an accumulation of dealing with conflict in an unhealthy manner over time, and now it has caught up with you.

How you deal with stressful situations is an accumulation of coping mechanisms you have used in past similar situations. God can still break the cycle, "cast your burden upon the LORD and He will sustain you" (Psalm 55:22).

Growth is always suppressed when there is an external weight applied to someone. There are emotional limitations on your productivity because you have something literally weighing you down. When you function beyond your level of tolerance, your relationships will be characterized by the fear of failure. Love will end up becoming a duty.

Take an inventory of your life, evaluate the triggers in your life, and surrender it to God. And when God has delivered you, find someone and "bear one another's burdens, and so fulfill the law of Christ" (Galatians 6:2). Life is better when we can share our joy and pain with others.

CONFLICT IS CONTACT, BUT NOT THE WAY YOU THINK

Where do the conflicts, and where do the quarrels among you come from? Is it not from this, from your passions that battle inside you? (James 4:1, NET)

We have conflict because of who we are. It's in our nature. It's inevitable that conflict will come, simply because conflict is contact.

An ethics professor asked his students to imagine a peaceful place. After allowing a couple of minutes to pass, he asked the students to share.

The first student raised his hand and said, "I was all alone in my grandfather's farmyard looking at the sunrays bringing to life the golden wheat fields as the wind moved them to and fro." That was the first student's peaceful place.

A mother of three raised her hand and ever so tenderly, she said, "It's that morning cup of coffee at 6 a.m. before the children and my husband are up, that's peaceful."

Another student added, "It's the day I stopped sharing my room with my sister, and my brother with his loud music moved out."

A common theme emerges as you listen to these students. Their descriptions of a peaceful place is a place that has no people. There's a false premise that peace is the absence of people. The contrary is true.

People bring peace into our lives just as they bring conflict. The two are inseparable because humans long for contact.

Peace is engaging people within your level of tolerance, and anything beyond your level of tolerance becomes conflict. In both cases, there is still human interaction. We get together based on our similarities. We grow because of our differences[20]. When two sides are trying to make a connection but failing to do it properly, conflict arises.

Avoidance of conflict is avoidance of connection.

Conflict has the potential to deepen our quality of connections because it takes us beyond our level of comfort

---

[20] Virginia Satir

When conflict comes, it has the potential to deepen our quality of connections because it takes us beyond our level of comfort. We grow better when our status quo is challenged. Sometimes it's a way of working out the kinks in the relationship.

Friends understand each other more after they resolve an issue.

Spouses bond further after a reconciliation.

Siblings are always at it, and that's why they say blood is thicker than water.

It doesn't always mean that love is absent. It's just a desire to connect but failing to do so appropriately.

When there is contact, friction occurs and bruises form. Hurt and pain can be a part of the process of contact. The scars we receive become a reminder of the attempts we made to connect, and the failure that came with it.

When pain and hurt have occurred, forgiveness becomes the only ointment to soothe the wound. When someone wrongs you, they create a debt, and the account needs to be settled.

Forgiveness can be quite costly. However, when the conflict has been resolved, the connection that can develop has the possibility of being stronger. Reconciliation creates mutual understanding of each other's tolerance of pain.

Forgiveness is a soothing ointment to the offended as well as to the offender. The opposite side is never responsible for making you forgive. Neither is the other side responsible for making you say, "I'm sorry." Forgiving and apologizing is never a response, but a pro-active initiative to build a better relationship.

> *Forgiving and apologizing is never a response, but a pro-active initiative to build a better relationship.*

There is a false premise that we forgive and forget. You might not forget the incident depending on the severity.

It might have been at a time when you needed the job the most, and you got fired for no fault of your own.

Your spouse should have known better, but they did it anyway.

Abuse of power by employers, parents, and community figures are all incidents that you will likely remember.

On my left arm just below my palm, I have a scar that I got as a little kid. I was sharpening a pencil with a sharp razor blade.

In one of the pull strokes as I removed the shavings of the pencil to expose the chalk, I sunk the blade too deep. I didn't pull it out fast enough before it reached my skin.

Blood gushed out, it hurt for several days and there was a deep scar. To this day, 20 plus years later, I still remember the incident. The scar is still there. However, there is no pain.

Forgiveness is like that. The scars will be there, but they won't hurt. You will remember the incident that caused the hurt, but the feelings of anger won't come up because you have forgiven.

You have let go of the debt that was owed to you. Conflict is contact, a deep human longing to be heard, to be seen and to belong.

When the tolerance level has been reached, forgiveness is the only way to bring things back to equilibrium. When we forgive, we heed God's call to "be kind to one another, tender-hearted, forgiving each other, just as God in Christ also has forgiven you" (Ephesians 4:32).

THE WAY OF THE GOSPEL

Conflict trains us to see the gospel afresh with new eyes over and over. In his book, *All Quiet on the Western Front*, Erich Remarque, a World War I veteran, describes an encounter between two enemy soldiers.

At the heat of the battle, a German soldier took shelter in a ditch. Looking around, he saw a wounded man who was dying. As he looked closer, he observed the man was wearing the enemy's uniform.

The German soldier's heart went out to him, and with hesitation, he inched closer while on high alert, in case it was a trap. As he got closer to the enemy soldier, he realized he was on his last dying breath. Seeing the sight of the man, he let his guard down and attended to the man. He gave him water to quench his thirst, and within a few moments, the wounded man opened up. He spoke of his wife and children. And with all of his strength, the German soldier helped him find his wallet and take out pictures of his family to look at one last time.

In his last dying breath, the German soldier helped the man sit up against the side of the trench. He helped him get a sip of water and open his notepad to share some images of his family. The soldier didn't die alone.

He found a new friend who was an enemy sworn to kill him. At that moment, the German soldier didn't see an enemy but a brother, a father, a husband, someone who loves and is loved. He saw someone just like him.

There's a certain kind of pessimism about mankind. People disappoint. They lie, cheat, and steal. Even those that you give your trust. We are a broken people, chained to our undesirable past. And you wonder, how will I make it? The gospel has a way.

The main thrust of the gospel is reconciliation. Before, "you who were once far away from God. You were his enemies, separated from him by your evil thoughts and actions" (Colossians 1:21, NLT). This was the status of the human condition before God's grace moved. It is this grace that gives us a new chance at life.

No one is beyond redemption. The greatest lie anyone has ever heard is that a relationship is not worth saving.

> *The greatest lie anyone has ever heard is that a relationship is not worth saving*

TAKE IF FROM JESUS, THOUGH:

"he was God, he did not think of equality with God as something to cling to. Instead, he gave up his divine privileges; he took the humble position of a slave and was born as a human being. When he appeared in human form. And being found in appearance as a man, he humbled himself by becoming obedient to death-- even death on a cross!" (Philippians 2:6, NLT)

No relationship is beyond God's reach. Jesus can restore the broken pieces. The final word rests with him.

GROW!

1. What baggage have you been carrying that has shaped the way you respond to people who see things differently than you?
2. Are you vying to be heard at the cost of losing your integrity?
3. Did you know the other side is not responsible for making you say sorry?

8

Changing the Odds

"Failure is not a destination, but a process in a journey to success."

FAILURE IS NOT FINAL.

Vincent Van Gogh's work sells for unprecedented prices, and are some of the most valuable and highly sought after in the world. One of his famous portraits was Dr. Gachet, which sold for a staggering price of $82.5 million in 1990 ($154.8 million today)[21], earning its place as one of the most expensive paintings ever sold. Van Gogh has gained world recognition in the world over the years.

---

[21] Doug Firebaugh

It wasn't always so during his time. Van Gogh was a failed and desperately starving artist. At the age of 37, Van Gogh committed suicide after suffering from mental illness and further depression because of his lack of success. During his lifetime, it is recorded that he produced more than 2,000 works of art, but only 2 paintings were sold[22]. His paintings, filled with emotion and passion, were not popular during his lifetime. However, his paintings would go on to influence a new generation of artists. To date, his works remain some of the most highly regarded paintings in modern art.

We all have sought to be competent in the many relationships we have. Each time we seem to get a handle of things, it feels like the rule book keeps on being changed.

Failure doesn't have to be final.

It's easy to feel like Adam and Eve. They had failed their creator, and on that dreadful day, they heard God calling in the Garden of Eden, "Where are you?"

Adam and Eve felt their nakedness by being away from God. They had wandered away physically, spiritually, and not to mention emotionally. A wall was built between God and the

---

[22] The Editors of Encyclopaedia Britannica. (2019, October 21). Vincent van Gogh: https:// www.britannica.com/biography/Vincent-van-Gogh

couple. The weight of guilt and shame weighed heavily on them.

God doesn't create in straight lines. Look at the splendour of his creations, animals, mountains, trees, and grass that blankets the hillside. Nothing is created straight, including humans-you and I. There is room for faults and growth. God works with imperfection. The so-called imperfections are his masterpiece works in the making. *You are his masterpiece.*

Manoah's wife was barren, and the birth of their son Samson, came in response to a desperate need to deliver Israel from the Philistines. Dedicated to the cause of God, Samson was supposed to be a "Nazirite to God from the womb". He was to "deliver Israel from the hands of the Philistines" (Judges 13:5). God confirmed that this was true twice, first to Manoah's wife and second directly to Manoah. A son was born, and his name was Samson. Samson was to be a nation's hope.

He was to set loose the chains that had kept Israel in bondage and fear.

The hand of God was going to be over him.

Since he was a Nazarite, he was to abstain from alcohol, cutting his hair, and having any contact with a dead body. His strength rested in obedience to God's command to not cut his hair. If the locks of his hair were uncut, he maintained the power of God.

The Philistines ceased to plunder Israel. There was peace once again; Samson became the champion of the people. His mighty deeds were heralded by the people and he became the deliverer of Israel.

Samson fell in love with a Philistine woman. One day on his way to see his lover, a lion jumped out to attack him, but "he tore him as one would tear a young goat, though he had nothing in his hand" (Judges 14:5). The same woman that he was in love with and determined to marry, was given over to his friend.

Heartbroken, Samson "went and caught three hundred foxes, and took torches, and turned *the foxes'* tail to tail and put one torch in the middle between two tails" (Judges 15:4). The foxes ran and lit the Philistines' grain.

Again, the Philistines tried to ambush Samson, and Samson "found a fresh jawbone of a donkey...and killed a thousand men with it (Judges 15:15).

Such were Samson's heroic acts; He became so comfortable and accustomed to victory after victory. Failure was a foreign concept to Samson.

Samson seemed to be taken with a Philistine woman.

He started meddling with another Philistine woman named Delilah.

Delilah became his weakness.

After he confessed where his strength lay, the Philistines soldiers came to capture him. With the anticipation that "I will go out as at other times and shake *himself* free" (Judges 16:20; emphasis added). Only this time, he was met with a chilling reality that the "Lord had departed from him."

Samson broke all his vows.

He touched a dead body, drank from the vine, and told Delilah the secret Nazarite.

Samson was taken captive in the dungeon of the Philistines, with his eyes gouged out. They called for him to be a spectacle for guests.

Once, he was a feared enemy.

Now he is blind and powerless.

As he leaned on two pillars that held the frame of the whole building, he remembered his maker and called to the Lord, "O Lord God, please remember me and please strengthen me just this time" (Judges 16:28). On that day, when he regained his strength and pushed the two pillars, "the dead whom he killed at his death were more than those whom he killed in his life."

Despite the odds, Samson accomplished more than he did on his last day. After his eyes were gouged out by his oppressor, all strength gone, failure would have been final. But God was not done with him. God was still going to accomplish his purpose through him.

Maybe unlike Samson, you've had a string of failure, and you are about to throw in the towel.

When Michael Jordan was asked how he rose to be a household name, his response was atypical,

I've missed more than 9000 shots in my career.

I've lost almost 300 games,

I've been trusted to take the game-winning shot 26 times, but I missed.

I've failed repeatedly in my life.

That is why I succeed.

Failure is not a destination, but a process in a journey to success. You are not defined by the one or two incidents that have left you down on your back.

When Jesus walks with you, every step becomes a learning opportunity to be ready when the same situation arises. Success belongs to Jesus! Therefore, if you want to experience relational success, you too must belong to Him.

Failure is not a destination, but a process in a journey to success.

Our secrets of shame that lurk in darkness are broken when they are brought into the light. We cannot ask God to transform us without first surrendering everything to His victorious power.

Failure is not final. Failure is being unprepared to deliver and not an indicator of self-worth; an unhappy process is not an unhappy ending.

Touched by God

Terry Swanson tells a story when he was young, during a time when he still had to share his room with his sister, Kathy.

One night after they both had been put to bed, but sleep hadn't claimed them yet, they played a little bit, told stories, and made animal noises—quietly though, because they didn't want to disturb Momma in her room right next to them.

She was ill—very ill.

Finally, stories started to run out, they paused and lay quietly for a while. Kathy broke the silence with a spiritual insight,

"Let's pray to Jesus and ask Him to make Momma well!"

"Great idea!"

Because of gravity of their mother's situation, Terry says, they prayed a long prayer, using as many important words as they could come up with.

When they had finished, he asked his sister if she thought that God heard them. Being that she was three years older than him, Terry felt she was more experienced in these matters. She, in turn, thought for a moment.

"I know! Let's ask God to touch us! Then we'll know for sure that He heard us!"

So, they stretched their arms up as high as they could. Not sure how long, but they laid there with their arms outstretched. Eventually, they fell asleep. God never touched his hand.

Momma never got healed.

Terry grew up and saw how absent God was in people's lives. No matter how much he reached out for a touch of love and affirmation, he never felt anything. And so, he rejected God throughout his young years.

In a testimony years later, Terry related his experience with God.

"God did touch me! I had not realized the reality of the Gospel—that it's all about a person who loves me and has forgiven me of everything. It's all about Him coming to get me and bringing me back into His arms and into a relationship with Him. It is then I felt the touch that I longed for."

There is one more death that changed the odds for all of humanity. Samson "killed at his death … more than those whom he killed in his life" (Judges 16:30).

Jesus too, while hanging on the cross, his death brought forth more to life than he did while he walked on earth.

Jesus truly came with the power of the Spirit to

"preach the gospel to the poor…

to proclaim release to the captives,

And recovery of sight to the blind,

To set free those who are oppressed,

To proclaim the favourable year of the Lord." (Luke 4:18-19)

Jesus wants to change your odds. To have healthy relationships, the first relationship that needs to be changed is your relationship with Jesus.

> *To have healthy relationships, the first relationship that needs to be changed is your relationship with Jesus*

It's time to move from barely making it. This is an invitation to thrive. This is an invitation to healthy relationships with Jesus at the center of them all.

GROW!

Have you surrendered to God?

About the Author

Kingsley Moyo is a Professional Counsellor, Pastor, and International Speaker. With over 20 years of experience in serving God from an early age when, Kingsley understands healthy relationships don't happen by chance.

Kingsley lives in Alberta, Canada with his wife and two children. He also pastors a dynamic church in Alberta. Kingsley is passionate about teaching on issues that affect people and relationships, helping individuals, couples, and families thrive one at a time. He is currently in pursuit of a Master of Arts in Marriage & Family, he holds a BA in Theology, and an Advanced Diploma of Applied Psychology, & Counselling.

THE R FACTOR

Acknowledgements

I don't know where to even begin. This book has been a journey of growth and discovery. There are many people who made this book possible. First, my wife, Sesu, who took care of things while I stayed up late. She encouraged me and entertained my crazy ideas, through and through you believed in me. Thank you for being supportive of my journey and passion.

Arnold Tshuma, my brainstorming chalkboard, nothing was impossible. Thank you for being passionate and sometimes more passionate than me.

Jome Sumiller, I always look better when you take my pictures. Thank you for the back cover photo.

Lulu Mashonganyika, thank you for encouraging me to see no limits and to keep moving to the next level.

To my writing coach, Jonathan Geraci, you left nothing out. Sometimes it took me time to catch on, thanks for showing me open doors and encouraging me.

Yumi Samson, thank you for giving this project detailed eyes. Thank you!

My siblings, Jasper, Sipho and mother, Dawn —you have been building blocks in shaping who I am. Thank you all for the part you played in making this book a success. To my launch team and to you who is going to purchase the book, Thank you!

Praise be the name of our Lord and Saviour Jesus Christ who has redeemed us by his grace. The one who loves more than any. 'God forbid that I should boast of anything but the cross of our Lord Jesus Christ' (Galatians 6:14, NEB).

www.ingramcontent.com/pod-product-compliance
Lightning Source LLC
LaVergne TN
LVHW020933090426
835512LV00020B/3344